BUSINESS ECONOMICS IN A RAPIDLY-CHANGING WORLD

SMALL BUSINESS TAX COMPLIANCE

BURDENS AND IRS RESPONSE EFFORTS

BUSINESS ECONOMICS IN A RAPIDLY-CHANGING WORLD

Additional books in this series can be found on Nova's website under the Series tab.

Additional e-books in this series can be found on Nova's website under the e-book tab.

BUSINESS ECONOMICS IN A RAPIDLY-CHANGING WORLD

SMALL BUSINESS TAX COMPLIANCE

BURDENS AND IRS RESPONSE EFFORTS

SHERI PATTON
EDITOR

nova publishers
New York

Library of Congress Cataloging-in-Publication Data

ISBN: 978-1-63484-565-6

Published by Nova Science Publishers, Inc. † New York

CONTENTS

Preface		**vii**
Chapter 1	Small Businesses: IRS Considers Taxpayer Burden in Tax Administration, but Needs a Plan to Evaluate the Use of Payment Card Information for Compliance Efforts *United States Government Accountability Office*	**1**
Chapter 2	Opening Statement of Steve Chabot, Chairman, House Committee on Small Business. Hearing on "How Tax Compliance Obligations Hinder Small Business Growth"	**71**
Chapter 3	Statement of Troy Lewis, Vice President, Heritage Bank. Hearing on "How Tax Compliance Obligations Hinder Small Business Growth"	**73**
Chapter 4	Statement of Stephen F. Mankowski, Partner, EP Caine & Associates, LLC. Hearing on "How Tax Compliance Obligations Hinder Small Business Growth"	**87**
Index		**93**

PREFACE

A challenge the Internal Revenue Service (IRS) faces is balancing efforts to minimize taxpayer burden with efforts to ensure compliance with the tax code. Small businesses are a vital source of economic growth in the United States. Reducing their costs for complying with the tax code may free up resources to expand, hire new employees, and contribute to the growth of the U.S. economy. This book describes characteristics of the small business population; describes how characteristics of a small business affect compliance burden; describes how IRS integrates small business compliance burden considerations in decision-making; and assesses IRS's plan for evaluating its payment card pilot.

In: Small Business Tax Compliance
Editor: Sheri Patton
ISBN: 978-1-63484-565-6

Chapter 1

SMALL BUSINESSES: IRS CONSIDERS TAXPAYER BURDEN IN TAX ADMINISTRATION, BUT NEEDS A PLAN TO EVALUATE THE USE OF PAYMENT CARD INFORMATION FOR COMPLIANCE EFFORTS*

United States Government Accountability Office

WHY GAO DID THIS STUDY

A challenge IRS faces is balancing efforts to minimize taxpayer burden with efforts to ensure compliance with the tax code. Small businesses are a vital source of economic growth in the United States. Reducing their costs for complying with the tax code may free up resources to expand, hire new employees, and contribute to the growth of the U.S. economy. GAO was asked to examine small business tax compliance burden and IRS's payment card pilot that addresses taxpayer non- compliance. This report: (1) describes characteristics of the small business population (2) describes how characteristics of a small business affect compliance burden; (3) describes how

* This is an edited, reformatted and augmented version of the United States Government Accountability Office publication, GAO-15-513, dated July 2015.

IRS integrates small business compliance burden considerations in decision-making; and (4) assesses IRS's plan for evaluating its payment card pilot. To answer these objectives, GAO analyzed Treasury and IRS data, research, and other documentation and interviewed agency officials. GAO used its guidance on program design evaluation to assess IRS's payment card pilot evaluation plan.

What GAO Recommends

To improve the evaluation of the payment card pilot, GAO recommends that IRS clearly define the stages of the pilot and establish measurable goals for determining when the pilot progresses from one stage to the next and develop an evaluation plan for the overall pilot that includes evaluation questions, complete descriptions of needed data, and evaluation criteria. IRS agreed to take the recommended actions.

What GAO Found

According to estimates produced by government tax researchers using 2010 taxpayer data, small businesses (defined in the research as individuals or entities with substantive business activity but with less than $10 million in total income and deductions) make up 99 percent of all businesses. Approximately 69 percent of small businesses (about 16 million) are individual taxpayers who report business income and the remaining 31 percent (or roughly 7.3 million) are partnerships or corporations. Small businesses with at least one employee make up about 20 percent of the small business population, but produce about 71 percent of total small business income.

Small businesses undertake a number of tax compliance-related activities that create burden. These activities can be grouped into general categories such as income tax activities, employer-related tax activities, and third-party information reporting activities. The tax compliance burden associated with these activities varies depending on the businesses' asset size, filing entity type (e.g., sole proprietor, partnership), number of employees, and industry type. According to IRS research, compliance burden increases with the size of businesses, whether measured in terms of assets, receipts, or employment. IRS also measured money and time burden as a portion of total business receipts, total assets, and burden per employee. Across all three measures, IRS results were consistent with the assumption that small businesses face significant fixed compliance costs combined with decreasing marginal costs as the business grows.

IRS's decision-making framework for administering the tax system includes consideration of small business compliance burden. For example, IRS's strategic plan identifies reducing taxpayer burden as a strategic goal. IRS provided examples of how it works with internal and external stakeholders to reduce taxpayer burden on small businesses. For example, IRS collaborated with Treasury and external stakeholders to develop a simplified method for some small businesses to calculate a home office deduction, which was introduced in January 2013. Previously, businesses had to complete a complex property depreciation calculation.

To improve tax compliance among small businesses, in 2012, IRS began piloting a program that compares payment data from payment settlement entities (such as credit card companies) with income reported by small businesses. IRS is testing ways to use payment data to detect underreporting of taxable income while minimizing small business taxpayer burden. While IRS's plans for evaluating the pilot include many key evaluation elements that GAO identified, other elements are missing. For example, IRS has defined high level pilot goals such as improving voluntary compliance and reducing the tax gap, but has not established measures for determining progress against these goals. Additionally, the plan did not adequately document evaluative questions, data collection needs, or the evaluative criteria necessary to assess whether pilot activities produced the intended results. Without these and other elements, IRS cannot ensure it is making evidence-based decisions about expanding and integrating pilot activities into broader small business compliance improvement efforts.

ABBREVIATIONS

CEAP	Correspondence Examination Assessment Project
FICA	Federal Insurance Contributions Act
FTE	full-time equivalent
FUTA	Federal Unemployment Tax Act
IRS	Internal Revenue Service
OTA	Department of Treasury – Office of Tax Analysis

RAS	Office of Research, Analysis, and Statistics
SB/SE	Small Business and Self-Employed Division
SOI	Statistics of Income
Treasury	Department of the Treasury

***

June 30, 2015

The Honorable Steven Chabot
Chairman
Committee on Small Business
House of Representatives

The Honorable Sam Graves
House of Representatives

Small businesses are a vital component of economic growth and job development in the United States. Although no single definition of a small business exists, one common characteristic used to identify a small business is number of employees. Businesses employing fewer than 100 people accounted for a little more than 34 percent of U.S. employment in 2012. Businesses with fewer than 500 employees accounted for more than 48 percent.[1] Like all businesses, small businesses face compliance burdens as a result of the tax code. Given the important role small businesses play in U.S. employment and overall economic progress, reducing the cost of compliance may free up resources to expand, hire new employees, and further contribute to the growth of the U.S. economy.

While limiting compliance burden is important, we have also reported that small businesses are a key contributor to the annual tax gap—the difference between taxes owed and taxes paid on time.[2] The Internal Revenue Service (IRS) most recently estimated the U.S. tax gap to be $450 billion for 2006. Nearly 40 percent, or $179 billion, of the tax gap can be attributed to the underreporting of business income tax on individual income tax returns, and by extension the underreporting of self- employment tax, which is largely assessed on the same business income for self-employed taxpayers. An additional 4 percent of the tax gap, or $19 billion, can be attributed to small corporations, which IRS defines as having less than $10 million in assets. One challenge IRS faces is balancing efforts to encourage voluntary tax compliance through reducing taxpayers' costs of compliance with enforcement efforts to address noncompliance.

Beginning in 2011, IRS began receiving new information that could help improve voluntary compliance. Under a 2008 law, payment settlement entities such as credit card companies and third-party network payers like PayPal began reporting to IRS the gross payments they process for each participating merchant on IRS Form 1099-K, *Merchant Card and Third Party Network Payments*.[3] In 2012, IRS began a payment card pilot to research and test ways to use Form 1099-K data to most effectively and efficiently improve voluntary compliance, detect noncompliance, and minimize burden on taxpayers.

You asked us to examine small business tax compliance burden and IRS's payment card pilot. This report: (1) describes the characteristics of the small business population; (2) describes how characteristics of a small business affect compliance burden; (3) describes how IRS integrates small business compliance burden considerations into decision making; and (4) assesses IRS's plan for evaluating its payment card pilot.

We used estimates from researchers at the U.S. Department of the Treasury (Treasury), Office of Tax Analysis (OTA) to describe general characteristics of the small business population, such as the number of small businesses and total income.[4] We examined IRS, academic, and other research on small business tax compliance burden to identify how small business characteristics affect compliance burden. We reviewed IRS's strategic plan and other relevant documents, and interviewed agency officials about various burden reduction decisions and initiatives. We obtained the perspectives of the small business community through literature reviews, document reviews, and interviews. We used criteria from our prior reports on program design and evaluation to assess IRS's plan for evaluating the payment card pilot.[5]

We conducted this performance audit from July 2014 to June 2015 in accordance with generally accepted government auditing standards. Those standards require that we plan and perform the audit to obtain sufficient, appropriate evidence to provide a reasonable basis for our findings and conclusions based on our audit objectives. We believe that the evidence obtained provides a reasonable basis for our findings and conclusions based on our audit objectives.

BACKGROUND

Identifying the Small Business Population

A consensus does not exist on a definition of small business, including which specific attributes or thresholds distinguish small businesses from other firms. Estimates of the small business population are driven by the purpose, concepts, and data that are used to produce the estimates. As we have previously reported, various thresholds such as number of employees, gross receipts, and number of shareholders may be used when determining which provisions of the tax code apply to a small business.[6]

In this report, we rely on studies that use taxpayer data for individuals and entities that generate business income. Businesses (including small businesses) file specific tax forms based on certain attributes of the business, such as the ownership structure and how the business income is taxed. Below are different types of businesses and the required forms and schedules.

- Nonfarm sole proprietorships (Form 1040, Schedule C) are unincorporated and owned by a single individual. Net business income or loss is included in the owner's individual adjusted gross income.
- Landlords (Form 1040, Schedule E-Part I) are individuals who report rental real estate activity on Part I of Schedule E.
- Farmers (Form 1040, Schedule F or Form 4835) are individuals who report farm income or landowners who report farm rental income.
- C corporations (Form 1120) are owned by shareholders. Corporate income is taxed at the corporate level on taxable income and at the shareholder level on distributed profits.
- S corporations (Form 1120-S) cannot have more than 100 shareholders, among other requirements. Gross income is distributed to shareholders and taxed at the shareholder level.
- Partnerships (Form 1065) are unincorporated businesses that have two or more owners. Profits and losses are distributed to owners who are taxed at the partner level.

IRS has separate operating divisions that focus on different types of taxpayers—individuals, small businesses and self-employed, large businesses, and tax exempt organizations. The Small Business and Self- Employed division oversees taxpayers filing tax returns as individuals with business income and as businesses with less than $10 million in total assets. However, not all of these tax returns are for business entities. This is because the principal purpose of some entities that file tax returns reporting business income may not be to generate revenue or to engage in substantive business activity. For example, some C corporations can serve as investment vehicles that engage in little or no business activity. Further, partnerships may be created to redistribute profits generated by another partnership and may not generate income themselves.[7] Filers of Form 1040, Schedule C, may be independent contractors who may more closely resemble employees rather than small businesses. Additionally, rental income for some individuals may be incidental and not represent business activities.

Small Business Tax Compliance Burden

We define tax compliance burden as the time and money spent by the taxpayer to meet tax obligations. This would include federal, state, and local obligations. This does not include tax liability. For the purposes of this report, we are only examining compliance burden as a result of federal tax obligations.[8] Time spent on tax activities can include working with a paid professional, tax planning, keeping records, completing forms, submitting forms, learning tax laws, and working with IRS on tax issues. Monetary burden can include expenses for hiring a paid professional to file taxes, investing in a tax software system, paying for payroll services, and legal fees. When measuring tax compliance burden, researchers may separate burden into both time and money, or they may place a value on the time spent by taxpayers and add it to monetary burden to create a single measure of tax compliance burden.[9] A key concept in tax administration is minimizing burden, including eliminating unnecessary burden.

MOST SMALL BUSINESSES ARE INDIVIDUALS, BUT MOST SMALL BUSINESS INCOME IS EARNED BY PARTNERSHIPS AND CORPORATIONS

As shown in figure 1, using data from researchers at Treasury's Office of Tax Analysis (OTA), most small businesses (approximately 69 percent or 16 million) are individual taxpayers who report business income on their Form 1040, using Schedule C (sole proprietor), Schedule E-Part I (landlords), or Schedule F (farmers).[10] The remaining 31 percent of small businesses (or roughly 7.3 million) are partnerships, S corporations, or C corporations. OTA researchers also provide a total income measure, generally defined as the sum of all business income reported on tax returns, including gross receipts, rents, dividends, capital gains, royalties, and interest.[11] Individual small businesses generated only 23 percent (or $1.4 trillion) of the total income of all small businesses, whereas small business partnerships, S corporations, and C corporations accounted for the majority—77 percent (or about $4.5 trillion)—of total small business income.

When looking at the average total income for small businesses (total income divided by number of filers), partnerships, S corporations, and C corporations each generated more than $450,000 on average, while sole proprietors, farmers, and landlords reported income of about $100,000 or less on average. Figure 2 shows the estimated average total income by small business type.

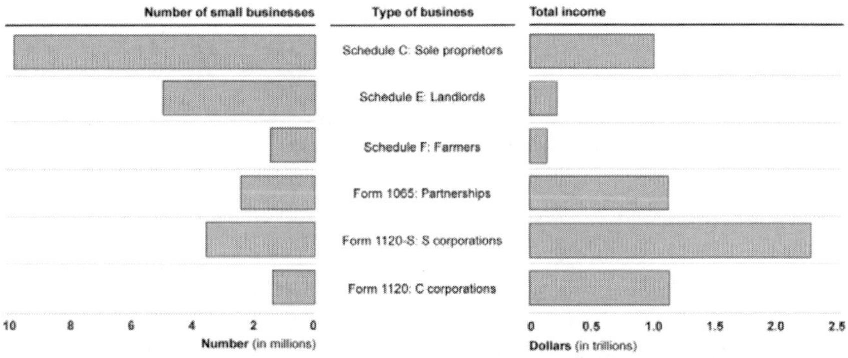

Source: Richard Prisinzano et al., "Identification of small Businesses Using Tax Data: 2010 Update" (presented at the 2013 National Tax Association's Spring Symposium, May 17, 2013). | GAO-15-513

Note: We refer to the estimated number of small business filers as the number of small businesses. The number of individual filers with business income includes taxpayers filing multiple schedules. Total income is generally defined as gross receipts, rents, dividends, capital gains, royalties, and interest. Total income for Schedule E filers is limited to rental real estate activity from Part I of that schedule. See appendix II for further discussion of the treatment of data used for this figure.

Figure 1. Estimated Number and Total Income by Type of Small Business (2010).

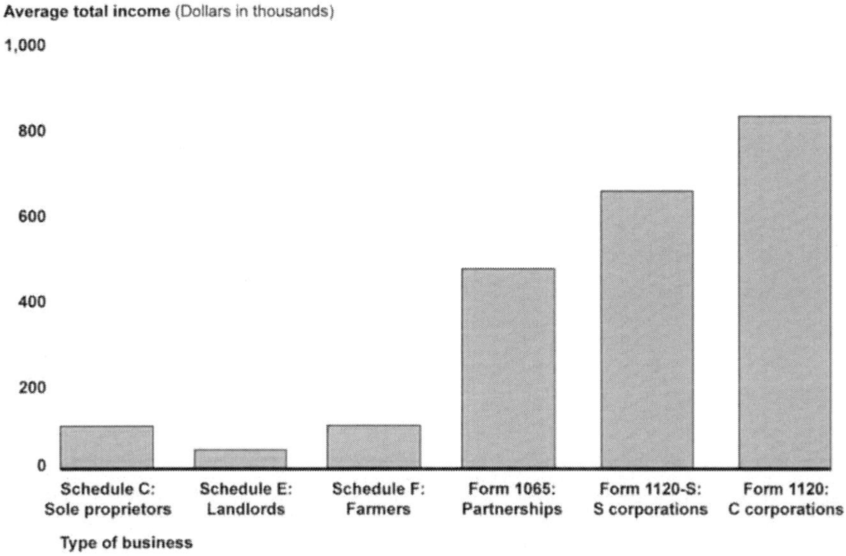

Source: Richard Prisinzano et al., "Identification of small Businesses Using Tax Data: 2010 Update" (presented at the 2013 National Tax Association's Spring Symposium, May 17, 2013). | GAO-15-513

Note: The average total income per small business is the ratio of total income and the number of filers for each type of business. We refer to the estimated number of small business filers as the number of small businesses. The number of individual filers with business income includes taxpayers filing multiple schedules. Total income is generally defined as gross receipts, rents, dividends, capital gains, royalties, and interest. Total income for Schedule E filers is limited to rental real estate activity from Part I of that schedule. See appendix II for further discussion of the treatment of data used for this figure.

Figure 2. Estimated Average Total Income by Type of Small Business (2010).

About 99 Percent of Businesses Report Total Income and Deductions of Less Than $10 Million

Small businesses (as defined as reporting total income and deductions of less than $10 million) make up 99 percent of the taxpayers identified as being engaged in substantial and substantive business activity.[12] For each type of filer, small businesses account for at least 95 percent of businesses. Among individual filers reporting business income, small businesses account for most of the reported income. However, among S corporations, C corporations, and partnerships, larger businesses account for most of the reported income, even though they are far outnumbered by small businesses, as shown in figure 3. The estimated average total income across all types of small businesses is $250,000, while the average total income for larger businesses is estimated to be $121 million.

Most Small Business Income Is Generated by Employers, but Most Small Businesses are Not Employers

Small businesses with at least one employee (which we will refer to as employers) generated most of the reported total income for small businesses (or about 71 percent).[13] Employers account for about 86 percent of total income for small business C corporations and S corporations combined and about 55 percent for small business sole proprietors, farmers, and partnerships.

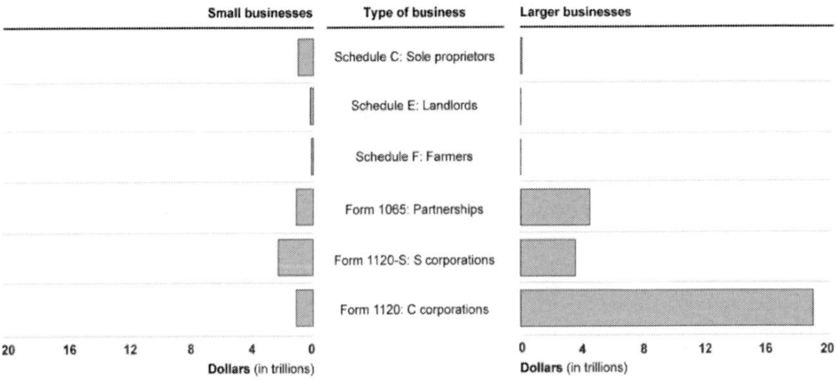

Source: Richard Prisinzano et al., "Identification of small Businesses Using Tax Data: 2010 Update" (presented at the 2013 National Tax Association's Spring Symposium, May 17, 2013). | GAO-15-513

Note: Total income is generally defined as gross receipts, rents, dividends, capital gains, royalties, and interest. Total income for Schedule E filers is limited to rental real estate activity from Part I of that schedule. Small businesses are defined as businesses that have $10 million or less in both total income and total deductions. Larger businesses are defined as businesses with more than $10 million in total income or total deductions. See appendix II for further discussion of the treatment of data used for this figure.

Figure 3. Estimated Total Income by Type for Small and Larger Businesses (2010).

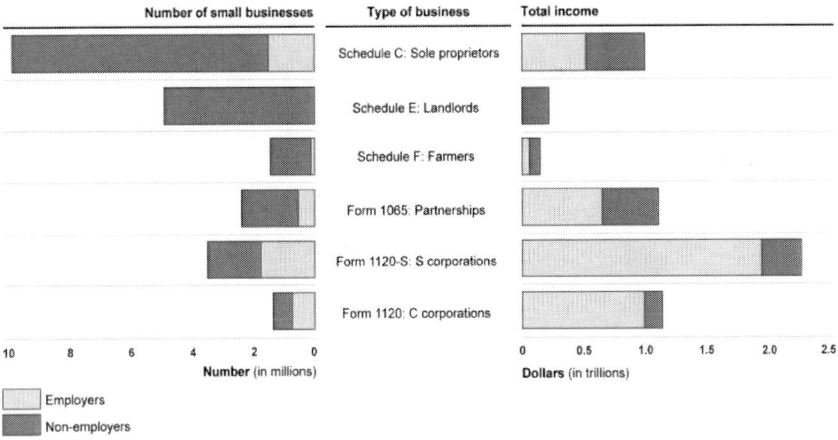

Source: Richard Prisinzano et al., "Identification of small Businesses Using Tax Data: 2010 Update" (presented at the 2013 National Tax Association's Spring Symposium, May 17, 2013). | GAO-15-513

Note: We refer to the estimated number of small business filers as the number of small businesses. The number of individual filers with business income includes taxpayers filing multiple schedules. Total income is generally defined as gross receipts, rents, dividends, capital gains, royalties, and interest. Total income for Schedule E filers is limited to rental real estate activity from Part I of that schedule. All Schedule E filers are defined to be non-employers, therefore no bars for employers appear in the above figure for Schedule E Landlords. See appendix II for further discussion of the treatment of data used for this figure.

Figure 4. Estimated Number of Small Businesses and Total Income by Employer and Non-Employer (2010).

Employers make up about 20 percent of all small businesses. Employers make up 16 percent of the combined group of small business Schedule C sole proprietors, Schedule F farmers, and partnerships and 51 percent of the combined group of small business C corporations and S corporations. Figure 4 shows the estimated number of small business filers and total income separated by employers and non-employers.

As shown in figure 5, employer small businesses, on average, generate more income than non-employer small businesses.

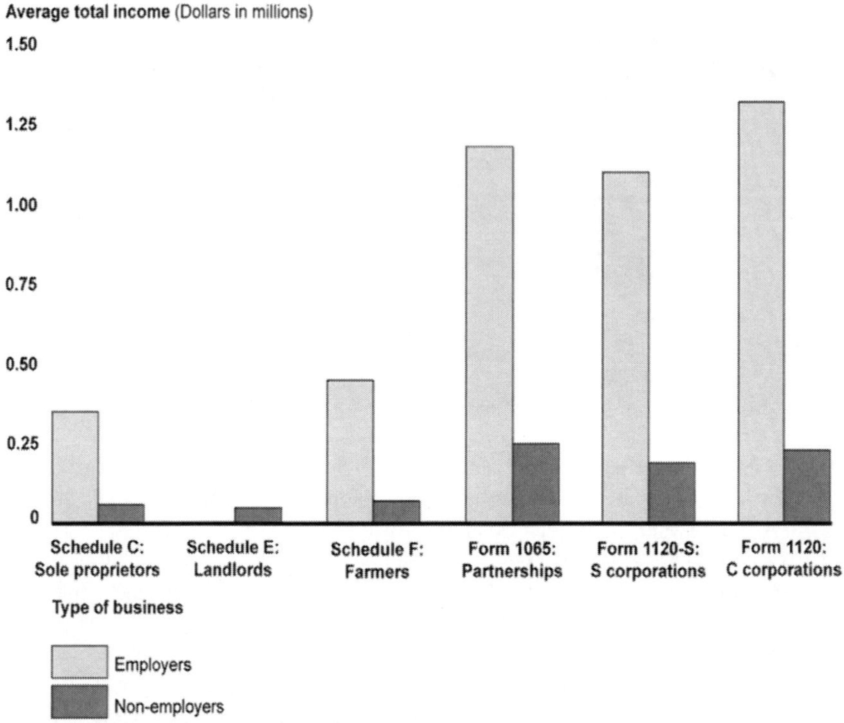

Source: Richard Prisinzano et al., "Identification of small Businesses Using Tax Data: 2010 Update" (presented at the 2013 National Tax Association's Spring Symposium, May 17, 2013). | GAO-15-513

Notes: The average total income per small business is the ratio of total income and the number of filers for each type of business. We refer to the estimated number of small business filers as the number of small businesses. The number of individual filers with business income includes taxpayers filing multiple schedules. Total income is generally defined as gross receipts, rents, dividends, capital gains, royalties, and interest.

Total income for Schedule E filers is limited to rental real estate activity from Part I of that schedule. All Schedule E filers are defined to be non-employers; therefore no bar for employers appears in the above figure for Schedule E Landlords. See appendix II for further discussion of the treatment of data used for this figure.

Figure 5. Estimated Average Total Income for Small Business by Employer and Non-Employer (2010).

Tax Compliance Burdens Vary Depending on a Small Business's Size, Number of Employees, Entity Type, Industry, and other Characteristics

Small businesses undertake a number of tax compliance-related activities that create burden.[14] These activities can be grouped into general categories:

- income tax activities,
- employer-related tax activities, and
- third-party information reporting and industry-specific tax activities.

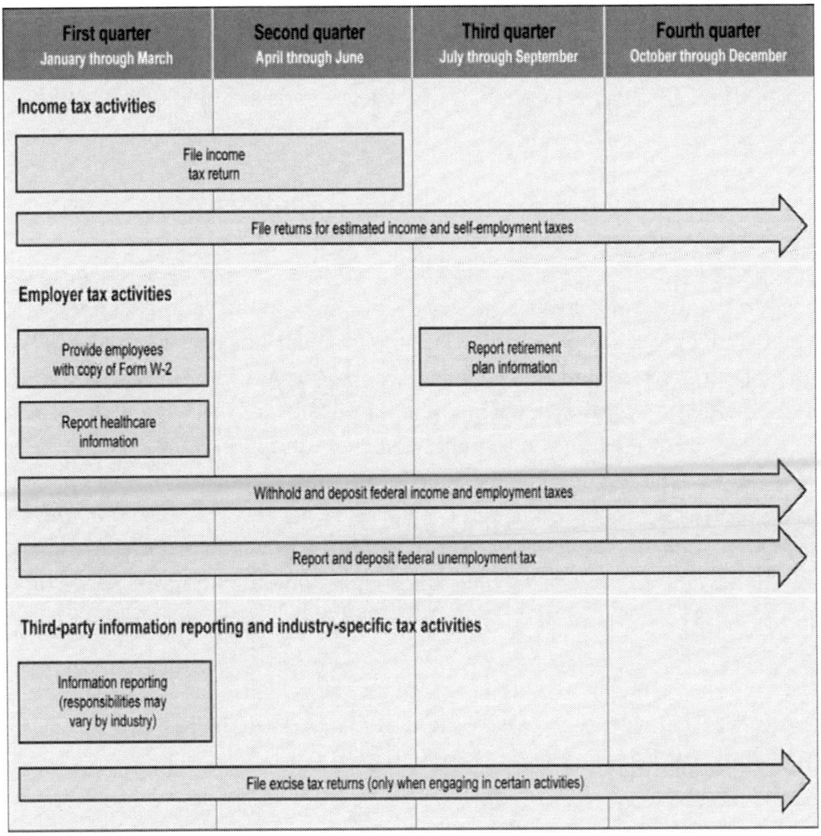

Source: GAO analysis of Internal Revenue Service (IRS) documents. | GAO-15-513

Figure 6. Overview of Tax Compliance Activities of Small Business Sole Proprietors.

The tax compliance burden associated with these activities varies by characteristics of the small business. Some of these characteristics include the business's asset size, filing entity type, number of employees, and industry type. Tax compliance activities are not limited to the annual filing of a tax return, but rather occur throughout the year. For example, sole proprietors are generally required to file income tax returns every April. Some small businesses need to pay estimated income taxes four times a year. Moreover, small businesses with employees are required to deposit employment taxes either monthly or semiweekly, and to report summary information of these activities on a quarterly basis. Additionally, depending on specific business operations, other tax compliance activities such as reporting excise tax, tax planning, and recordkeeping happen throughout the tax year. Figure 6 provides an overview of some of these tax compliance activities for sole proprietors and when they occur.

Appendix III, table 8 provides a more detailed description of tax activities.

Income Tax Activities, Such as Filing Income Tax Forms and Schedules, Vary by Small Business Type

Every year, small businesses need to file income tax returns and may pay estimated income taxes quarterly. The type of small business dictates the type of income tax returns and related schedules that need to be filed. Some of the returns include a set of schedules embedded in the form— found within the income tax return—while some small businesses and individuals with business income must attach a mandatory schedule to their return. For example, the primary corporate income tax return, Form 1120, *U.S. Corporation Income Tax Return*, contains eight embedded schedules, while sole proprietorships file Form 1040, *U.S. Individual Income Tax Return*, and attach Form Schedule C, *Profit or Loss from Business*.

Employer-Related Tax Activities, such as Withholding Employment Taxes, Depend on a Business's Number of Employees

Small businesses with employees are responsible for reporting, withholding, and depositing employment and unemployment taxes. While these requirements may impose a cost on employers, withholding is widely believed to improve compliance and may reduce compliance burdens for employees. The number of employment tax reports and deposits depends on the number of employees and the resulting employment tax liability owed at a particular time (see table 1). In general, businesses with an employment tax liability greater than $50,000 need to make deposits more frequently than businesses with a lower liability. Additionally, each year, the employer must furnish a copy of Form W-2, *Wage and Tax Statement*, to each employee. Since the characteristics of employers vary, responsibilities for withholding, depositing, and reporting employment taxes can differ. For example, consider a small business restaurant owner who has 20 employees and has an employment tax liability of less than $50,000. She files a Form 941 quarterly which details the income tax withholdings for each of her 20 employees. Since her liability is less than $50,000, she deposits these withholdings monthly. At the end of the year, she must complete 20 Forms W-2 to report wages, tips, and other compensation paid to each employee.

Table 1. Employment Tax Requirements

Type of employment tax	Primary return	Deposit
Personal income tax withheld[a] Social Security and Medicare tax withheld (the Federal Insurance Contributions Act tax, or FICA)	Form 941, *Employer's Quarterly Federal Tax Return*[b]	Monthly if liability ≤ $50,000 in lookback period— (last two quarters of previous tax year and first two quarters of the current tax year). Semiweekly if liability > $50,000 in lookback period. If $100,000 or more in taxes is accumulated on any day during a monthly or semiweekly deposit period it must be deposited by the next business day.
Federal Unemployment Tax Act (FUTA) tax	Form 940, *Employer's Annual Federal Unemployment (FUTA) Tax Return*	If FUTA tax is $500 or less in a quarter, carry it over to the next quarter. Continue carrying tax liability over until the cumulative tax is more than $500. At that point, it must be deposited for the quarter.

Source: GAO analysis of IRS documents. | GAO-15-513

Notes:

[a] For the purposes of the regulations governing deposit requirements, income tax withholding is generally considered an employment tax. 26 C.F.R. § 31.6302-1(e).

[b] Form 943, *Employer's Annual Federal Tax Return for Agricultural Employee*, is used by employers of agricultural workers.

Small businesses also report health care and retirement information. The information reported for these areas depends on a business's number of employees. The entity type also plays a role in the information reported about health care. Under the Patient Protection and Affordable Care Act, employers report the cost of coverage under an employer-sponsored group health plan on Form W-2. Beginning in January 2016, employers with 50 or more full-time employees will need to provide employees with a Form 1095-C, *Employer-Provided Health Insurance Offer and Coverage*. Some employers decide to offer pension plans and are responsible for reporting this information. While businesses must maintain records about these plans, most pension plans do not have any separate filing or reporting requirements with IRS. However, certain retirement plans offer small employers and self-employed individuals a deduction for contributions, and allows them to defer tax on income paid into the plan. To receive deductions, the small businesses must report this information to IRS using certain forms.

Third-Party Reporting Varies Depending on Business Size and Entity Type; Excise Tax Burden Is Industry Specific

Many businesses, including small businesses, are required to report on certain transactions they enter into with other entities. This is a form of third-party reporting. IRS uses this information to verify compliance by comparing the income or expenses reported by third parties to the income or expenses reported by small businesses on tax returns. Using Form 1099-MISC, small businesses report items such as rent payments and payments to nonemployees for services of at least $600, subject to certain exceptions. The burden created by this requirement grows with the size of the business because larger businesses would need to file more 1099-MISC forms. However, while a larger business may have more transactions, it may also have an accounting system designed to identify transactions of more than $600 that a smaller business might not have.

Another characteristic that affects third-party reporting requirements is entity type. For example, partnership entities are required to report the distributive shares of their partners on Schedule K-1. However, other entity types such as sole proprietorships do not have similar requirements.

Additionally, a small business may have many industry-specific requirements related to excise taxes. IRS administers several broad categories of excise taxes, including environmental taxes, communications taxes, fuel taxes, retail sale of heavy trucks and trailers, luxury taxes on passenger cars, and manufacturers' taxes on a variety of different products. For example, a small business in the trucking industry that makes deliveries over public highways is required to file Form 2290, *Heavy Highway Vehicle Use Tax Return*.

IRS's Compliance Burden Models' Estimates Provide Valuable Insights

IRS has developed several models to provide information for assessing the impact of the tax code and IRS programs on taxpayers. These models also help IRS assess the role of compliance burden and comply with requirements by the Office of Management and Budget for information on burden under the Paperwork Reduction Act.[15] In the past 15 years, IRS has developed a number of burden models for individual and business taxpayers—both small and large.[16]

Estimated Recordkeeping and Filing Burdens Vary with Characteristics of Businesses and Complexity of Returns

Estimates of business compliance burdens that IRS's models have produced over the years indicate that burdens increase with the size of businesses, whether measured in terms of assets, receipts, or employment; however burden per dollar of assets or receipts or per employee decline with size due to economies of scale. For example, a small business owner who does his own taxes may create a spreadsheet to compute the business's taxes and keep track of the employment taxes he owes for each employee. The effort the small business owner makes to build that spreadsheet is a fixed cost—a cost that does not change with an increase or decrease in the amount of goods or services that are produced. As the small business owner's sales grow and as he hires more employees, he doesn't have to repeat that effort; he just has the small additional cost of adding new data on income and employees to the spreadsheet. As this business grows, its total compliance costs decline both as a proportion of sales and on a per-employee basis. For these reasons, the costs per dollar of receipts or per employee are larger for small businesses than for larger ones.

IRS measured money and time burden as a portion of total business receipts, total assets, and burden per employee. Across all three measures, IRS results are consistent with the assumption that small businesses face significant fixed compliance costs combined with decreasing marginal costs as the business grows (see appendix III, tables 9 through 11).[17] When looking at total receipts and asset size across all businesses, estimated total monetized business compliance costs by business entity type varied depending on the type of entity and the entity's gross receipts. This variation is one reason why compliance burden on small businesses is a concern (see appendix III, table 12).

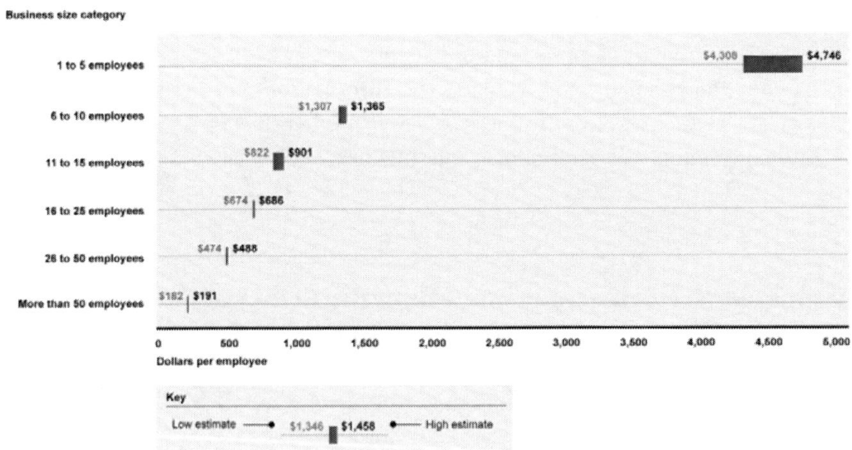

Source: Donald DeLuce et al., "Aggregate Estimates of Small Business Taxpayer Compliance Burden," *IRS Research Bulletin* (2007). | GAO-15-513

Note: Results include C corporations, S Corporations, and partnerships with assets totaling $10 million or less and do not include sole proprietorships. It is important to note that the imprecise nature of each size measure to accurately capture a taxpayer's size of business activities may exaggerate the ratio for the smaller-sized categories. For example, a business with low total assets and high total receipts would have a very different ratio of compliance burden per unit of size depending on which classification scheme is used. However, the general trend holds consistent across IRS measurements of size in that average burden decreases as the size of the business increases.

Figure 7. Estimated Tax Compliance Burden per Employee for S Corporations, C Corporations, and Partnerships (2002).

Figure 7 shows IRS's estimates of compliance costs per employee for S corporations, C corporations, and partnerships. According to the estimates, costs for corporations and partnerships with 1 to 5 employees range from $4,308 to $4,746, compared to $182 to $191 per employee for businesses with 50 or more employees. IRS conducted this research using 2002 taxpayer data. Estimates using more recent data have not been produced. A number of factors would likely affect these estimates if they were produced using current data, including inflation, accounting software improvements, and tax law changes.

Estimates from IRS's compliance burden models also show that burdens vary by industry. According to IRS, the retail trade industry incurs the largest pre-filing and filing time burden—businesses in this industry spent an average of between 325 and 331 hours per year on such activities. Manufacturing incurred the largest pre-filing and filing monetary burden, with businesses spending an average of $2,740 to $2,813 per year on these activities. Agriculture, forestry, and fisheries incurred the smallest average time spent on tax compliance activities (180 to 184 hours) and second smallest average compliance costs ($1,489 to $1,590).[18] Some industries have higher time and monetary compliance costs because the nature of those businesses may affect the complexity of tax activities. For additional information on industry burden, see table 13 in appendix III.

IRS and Treasury researchers have used both the business and individual taxpayer burden models to estimate the influence of specific business characteristics on compliance burdens. Their estimates suggest that recordkeeping and filing burdens increase as the volume of complex compliance activities undertaken by businesses increases, regardless of the size or other characteristics of those businesses. The results for the full population of individual taxpayers were similar.[19] Activities are categorized into varying levels of complexity based on an overall complexity of extracting information from the entity's financial books, items that may require a separate recordkeeping system or a process with potentially separate rules for each item, and tracking records across years.

IRS has not yet attempted to separately measure the compliance burden costs for small businesses associated with filing information returns. However, in a previous report, we found compliance cost per form decreased as the number of forms handled increases. Specifically, two information return preparers reported the cost per transaction for preparing and filing Forms 1099 with IRS of about $10 per form for 5 forms to about $2 per form for 100 forms, with one of them charging about $.80 per form for 100,000 forms.[20]

Audits and Other Compliance Contacts Can Be a Significant Source of Burden for Taxpayers, but Research Is Limited

IRS has not conducted research to estimate the compliance costs of audits and other post-filing compliance contacts for small businesses. However, IRS conducted preliminary research on compliance costs for individual filers that can provide some insights into the sources of burden that would affect some small businesses that report business income on individual tax returns. From the taxpayer perspective, post-filing begins when the taxpayer receives notice of an issue with an already filed tax return and concludes when the issue has been resolved. Post-filing compliance costs include any time spent on resolving an issue or money spent on things ranging from postage to paying a tax professional. IRS's preliminary data on individual post-filing compliance costs provide information on the time and money spent on post-filing activities such as an audit—a review of accounts and financial information to ensure information is being reported correctly—or collections—receiving a bill for not paying taxes in full when a tax return was filed.

For individual filers, IRS research indicates that the level of compliance costs are highly dependent on the approach IRS takes in how it contacts the taxpayer to address potential underreporting or underpayment of tax obligations. IRS's preliminary estimates, based on survey data from 2011, indicate that the average post-filing compliance costs were the highest for a field exam—an audit conducted at an individual's home or place of business—at $4,800, followed by office exam—an audit conducted at an IRS office—at $2,165. A notice informing the taxpayer that they did not report all of their earnings had the lowest estimated average post-filing compliance costs at $230. IRS's research on the magnitude of audit costs for individual filers likely includes individual filers who are small business owners. Those businesses are likely to have more complicated returns and, as a consequence, their burden is likely to be at least as great as the averages show for individual filers. For more details concerning post-filing compliance costs, see figure 13 in appendix III.

According to IRS, the audit rate for small business taxpayers is higher than the rate across all individual taxpayers because small businesses historically have higher noncompliance than other taxpayers.[21] Table 2 provides detailed information on the audit rates across small business types.

Table 2. Audit Rates Across Small Business Types (Fiscal Year 2014)

Business Category	Size	Audit Rate
Individual Nonfarm Business Returns[a]	Gross receipts < $25,000	1.0%
	Gross receipts $25,000 < $100,000	1.9%
	Gross receipts $100,000 < $200,000	2.4%
	Gross receipts $200,000 or more	2.1%
Individual Farm Business Returns[a]		0.5%
Individual Business Returns with total positive income of at least $200,000 and under $1,000,000[b]		2.7%
Small Corporations[c]	Total assets < $250,000	0.9%
	Total assets $250,000 < $1,000,000	1.2%
Partnerships[d]	Total	0.4%
S Corporations[d,e]	Total	0.4%

Source: IRS Data Book 2014. | GAO-15-513

Notes:

[a] Total gross receipts is the sum of gross receipts from farm and nonfarm businesses without earned income tax credit.

[b] Total positive income is the sum of all positive amounts shown for the various sources of income reported on the individual income tax return and, thus, excludes losses.

[c] Includes returns with assets of less than $10 million.

[d] Nontaxable returns are filed for entities that generally do not have a tax liability, but pass through any profits and losses to the underlying owners who include these profits or losses on their income tax returns.

[e] Includes most Forms 1120S, which are filed by qualifying S corporations electing to be taxed through shareholders.

While we did not examine post-filing costs, in a past report on correspondence audits, we found a number of issues which contribute to taxpayer compliance burden. These issues included IRS backlogs in responding to taxpayers who provide documentation in response to IRS's audit notices and unrealistic audit time frames set by IRS.

Table 3. General Guiding Principles and Items Employees Consider When Assessing Burden

Guiding Principle	Considerations
Leverage Technology	• Will a new requirement preclude the taxpayer's ability to e-file? • Is there an electronic submission alternative other than paper (e.g. web technology or e-mail)? • Can fillable forms be created?
Leverage Existing Data	• Are there opportunities to leverage information already being requested by another IRS function, government, or from accessible third-party data to limit the information collection burden on the taxpayer (inquire through web research, third parties, or impacted stakeholders)? • Are there opportunities to coordinate with third parties to reduce the burden to taxpayers in meeting the requirements (e.g., consolidate data collection resulting in one form versus two)?
Consider Pre-decisional Stakeholder Input	• Do the procedures/requirements conform to current external business processes or recording/reporting practices? • Are your documents in plain, coherent, and unambiguous terminology?
Benefit Must Outweigh Burden	• Are you requiring documentation that is not necessary to comply with the law and/or which may not actually be reviewed by IRS (or rarely reviewed)? • Are there consequences to the taxpayer for failing to provide the data? If not, how sure are we that they will provide accurate information? • If there are multiple options for legislative implementation, which options are expected to provide the greatest benefit to tax administration for the public cost imposed? • Can the procedure be optional versus mandatory? • Can a short form, or other simplified method, be created for some of the population? • Can a safe harbor procedure be offered to mitigate burden, especially for low income taxpayers and small businesses? • Can the frequency of information collection be limited/reduced? • Should transition relief be offered?

Source: IRS Internal Revenue Manual 2015. | GAO-15-513

IRS's Decision-Making Framework Includes Consideration of Small Business Compliance Burden

IRS's Strategic Goals and Internal Revenue Manual Describe the Agency-wide Approach to Taxpayer Burden Reduction

One of IRS's goals in its strategic plan is to deliver high quality and timely service to reduce taxpayer burden and encourage voluntary compliance.[22] Under this goal, IRS has identified seven objectives that further define how it intends to achieve the goal. One objective is to reduce taxpayer burden and increase return accuracy at filing through timely and efficient tax administration processing. IRS outlined performance measures for each strategic goal and objective in a supplement to its financial statement for fiscal years 2013 and 2014.[23] In this supplement, IRS describes some of the initiatives launched or continued and progress made in achieving performance goals. IRS also includes a discussion of goals missed. Several of these goals, if achieved, could have a positive impact on reducing small business compliance burden. For example, responding more quickly to telephone calls, correspondence, and requests for in-person service, as well as enhancing the online experience for customers, could benefit small businesses by requiring them to expend less time and fewer resources for IRS outreach.

In addition to the goals and objectives that focus on burden reduction in the strategic plan, IRS listed general guiding principles for reducing burden in the *Internal Revenue Manual 22.24.1 - IRS Servicewide Burden Reduction Activities*. The guiding principles are intended to support the consideration of compliance burden as part of tax administration. According to the manual, IRS carries out its mission to achieve significant reduction in unnecessary burden by considering taxpayer burden when implementing and reviewing policies and procedures. See table 3 for a list of the guiding principles.

According to the Internal Revenue Manual, the mission to reduce taxpayer burden and improve service is embedded in the IRS culture and a responsibility of all divisions. Though staffed to the Small Business and Self-Employed division, a senior advisor serves as the single point of contact for taxpayer burden reduction initiatives across all divisions. The manual states that this arrangement is intended to provide a link across the agency to ensure burden reduction is incorporated within decision- making frameworks. The advisor also acts as a liaison with external stakeholders.

IRS Has Worked with Internal and External Stakeholders to Identify and Reduce Small Business Tax Compliance Burden

IRS officials provided examples of efforts made to engage with internal and external stakeholders to reduce small business tax compliance burden. To engage internal stakeholders, employees can suggest ways to reduce burden by using Form 13285, *Taxpayer Burden Reduction Referral.* This form allows employees to note an issue causing taxpayer burden, describe the affected population, and propose a solution. Employees can also explain who needs to be involved in making the change, the resources needed, taxpayer benefits, compliance risks, and suggestions for how to measure burden reduction savings (e.g., reduced costs to the taxpayer or reduced costs to IRS). One notable example of a burden reduction initiative at IRS was developing a simplified method for determining the Office in the Home tax deduction.

Other internal activities include providing employees with an online burden risk estimator tool designed to aid employees in determining whether certain decisions about the design of tax forms for individuals (Form 1040 and associated schedules and forms) could impose significant burdens on taxpayers. This tool is an Excel spreadsheet that uses some of the data used in the more elaborate burden estimation models discussed previously in this report. The tool provides staff with an estimate of the number of taxpayers who would be affected by a specific potential tax form change, as well as a rough indication of whether the effect on compliance burden would be significant. Divisions can use this tool to identify decisions that merit more in-depth evaluations, potentially involving the full burden estimation model.

SIMPLIFIED OFFICE IN THE HOME DEDUCTION ILLUSTRATES HOW IRS CONSIDERS BURDEN WHEN IMPLEMENTING INITIATIVES

IRS officials offered an example of how the agency considered compliance burden principles when implementing new or changed tax laws or administrative procedures with the introduction of a simplified method for small businesses to calculate their Office in the Home Deduction. This method was introduced in 2013 and generally allows filers to receive a deduction of $5 per square foot of office space, up to a maximum area of 300 square feet. The alternative method involves a more complex calculation of property depreciation.

> Although the Department of the Treasury (Treasury) and IRS officials reported considering this proposal as early as 2006, in July 2012, Treasury and IRS redoubled their efforts in response to an Office of Management and Budget request to identify initiatives that would eliminate at least 2 million hours in annual burden. To meet this request, IRS reached out to employees and Senior Executive staff, and also reviewed prior submissions, form burden statistics, and other suggestions that had been considered in the past. The group reviewed the proposals and made a final determination that this initiative should be implemented. IRS officials told us that they considered burden and compliance risk within this decision-making process and discussed tradeoffs of their decisions. IRS received external stakeholder input from representatives of the small business community, such as the U.S. Chamber of Commerce and the National Federation of Independent Business, who have recognized this as a positive development. IRS said the process of working collaboratively across the organization, with external parties, and with Treasury allowed them to consider the interests and concerns of all parties. This helped IRS weigh tradeoffs of decisions that could affect both compliance and compliance burden.
>
> Source: GAO analysis of IRS information. | GAO-15-513

IRS undertakes a number of activities to engage external stakeholders such as providing information on its website and holding forums with small business representatives. IRS has a website page that defines taxpayer burden, provides links to submit ideas for burden reduction, and outlines how IRS selects burden reduction initiatives. Another example of IRS outreach to the small business community is the quarterly Small Business Forum. IRS officials told us that they use the information from these forums to inform their decision-making process for practices and policies that affect small businesses. For example, IRS used feedback from forum participants to refine the language used in burden surveys it administers to the business community, and used what was learned to inform its current burden models. Similar to internal stakeholders, external stakeholders can make burden reduction suggestions using Form 13285- A, *Reducing Tax Burden on America's Taxpayers (Referral Form for Use by the Public)*, which allows them to describe the issue causing taxpayer burden, the affected population, and the proposed solution.

Small Business Representatives We Spoke with Identified Areas That Contribute to Compliance Burden

We also interviewed small business representatives (external stakeholders) who acknowledged IRS's external stakeholder outreach efforts and how they have been effective in identifying opportunities to reduce compliance burden. However, they also described a number of areas where small business compliance burden could be further reduced.[24] These areas include issues related to IRS customer service, filing requirements, lack of or delayed official guidance, and compliance contacts. According to these representatives, when they call IRS, they can have long wait times, be disconnected, or be directed to IRS staff who are unable to provide the needed assistance. We have recently reported on these issues as well.[25]

Further, several representatives shared the perspective that complex filing requirements contribute to compliance burden. While small businesses sometimes anticipate significant tax relief through tax credits and deductions such as the small employer health care credit and mileage and vehicle deductions, some small businesses may not be claiming these credits due to the time, cost, and complexity associated with claiming them. One concern we heard from small business representatives was that after a tax practitioner expends resources to compile the necessary documentation and calculate the credit, their client (the small business) is ineligible to claim the credit. This could result in additional taxpayer burden if tax preparers bill their clients for calculating the credit when it is not claimed.

In addition to facing burdens due to new and complex tax provisions, representatives we spoke with also expressed concern over the compliance burden associated with delayed or missing official guidance, particularly for the Patient Protection and Affordable Care Act employer mandate.[26] Representatives also noted that deadlines for responding to certain IRS notices can be difficult for small businesses when the requested information is not readily available. We recognize that IRS is aware of many of these concerns and, through various initiatives, has made efforts to address these issues. However, continued attention to these areas will be key to effectively reducing burden.

We routinely issue reports on aspects of IRS's enforcement and administrative operations, some of which may impact small business tax compliance burden. In many cases we have made recommendations that, if implemented, could help to reduce these burdens. Selected recommendations that have yet to be implemented are listed in appendix IV.

IRS's Overall Evaluation of Its Payment Card Pilot has Several Strengths, but Does Not Fully Address All Elements Necessary to Effectively Assess Results

New Payment Card Data Provide Opportunities to Improve Voluntary Compliance and have Potential to Help IRS Better Identify Noncompliant Small Business Taxpayers

Beginning in tax year 2011, payment settlement entities were required to send IRS Forms 1099-K to report gross merchant payments in which a payment card or a third-party payment network was used as the form of payment.[27] Payment settlement entities report the gross amount of all reportable transactions a merchant made through them, for the calendar year, without regard to adjustments for credits, cash equivalents, discounts, fees, refunds, or other deductions.

A copy of the 1099-K is also sent to the taxpayer. The reporting of this information to both IRS and the taxpayer can encourage voluntary compliance by small businesses in at least two ways. First, since taxpayers know IRS is also receiving this income information, they are more likely to include it on their tax return. Second, taxpayers have another source of information they can use to help calculate or verify business income.

Payment card reporting also provides IRS with an information source it can use to compare against the income reported by small business taxpayers on their tax returns. As such, it can serve as a tool for identifying noncompliant taxpayers, including those who failed to file a tax return at all and those who underreported their income. This type of comparison is a common IRS enforcement technique. For example, IRS can directly compare information it receives on a taxpayer's Form W-2, *Wage and Tax Statement*, against a tax return to determine if the taxpayer reported earnings and withheld taxes correctly.

However, matching is more complicated for Forms 1099-K than Forms W-2 because IRS cannot directly match the line items on 1099-Ks to line items on tax returns. The Form 1099-K reports the gross amount of payment card and third party network transactions made through a payment settlement entity. This does not match the gross receipts line on tax returns because Form 1099-K transactions may include items like sales tax, gratuities, and cash back, all of which are not income. Furthermore, tax return gross receipts can include cash and check revenue, which is not captured on Form 1099-K. To leverage Form 1099- K data, IRS researched and tested ways in which the new data can be used to most effectively and efficiently improve voluntary compliance, detect noncompliance, and identify those who did not file returns.

The Payment Card Pilot includes six activities to test three methodologies for selecting cases, as described in table 4.

Table 4. Description of Payment Card Pilot Activities

Case selection methodology	Pilot program activities
Collection IRS uses Form 1099-K data to identify nonfiler taxpayers and taxpayers with unpaid assessments.	*Collection* IRS uses Form 1099-K information to identify nonfiler taxpayers, prioritize casework, and calculate taxpayer income.
Line by Line Comparison IRS compares Form 1099-K data with tax returns. A notice is sent if card receipts are greater than what the taxpayer	*Automated Underreporter* IRS compares the gross amount of the total reportable payment card/third-party network transactions for the calendar year to individual tax returns (Form 1040 Schedules C/E/F).
	Business Underreporter IRS compares the gross amount of the total reportable payment card/third party network transactions for the calendar year to business tax returns (Forms 1120, 1120S, and 1065).
Payment Mix Methodology IRS compares the relative cash and card revenues of similar businesses by setting thresholds for identifying	*Alternative Notice* IRS issues taxpayer a letter asking them to review their books and records to ensure all gross receipts are reported.
underreporters.	*Technical Audit* IRS tests the effectiveness of this compliance treatment using Form1099-K data in a correspondence audit.
	Field Audit IRS tests the effectiveness of this compliance treatment using Form1099-K data in a field audit.

Source: GAO analysis of IRS pilot documentation. | GAO-15-513

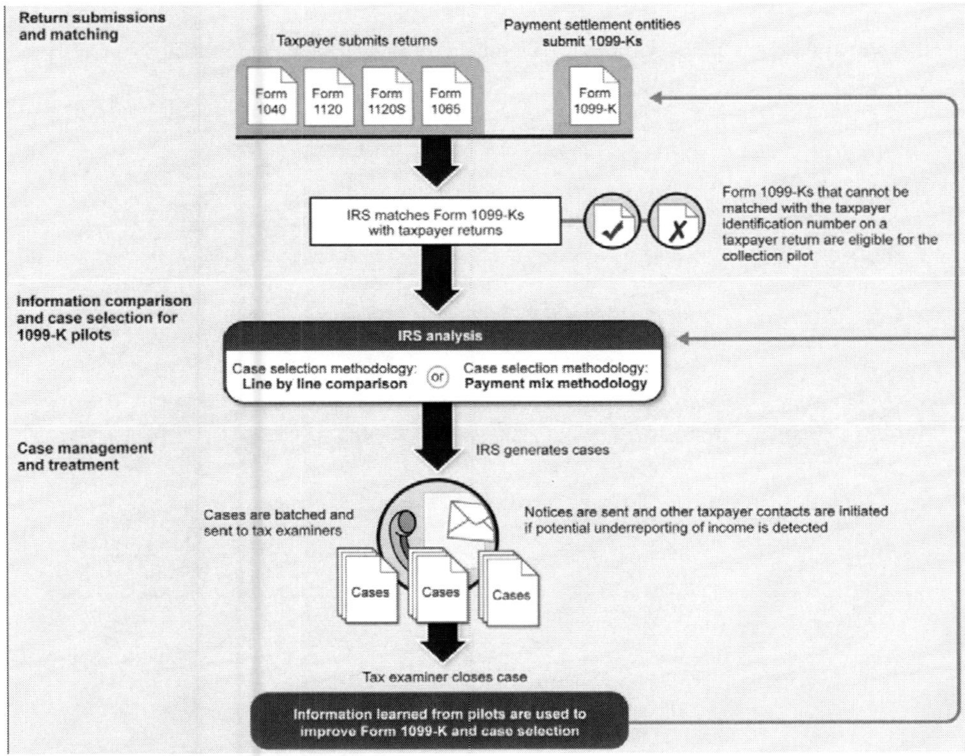

Source: GAO analysis of IRS pilot documentation. | GAO-15-513

Figure 8. IRS Form 1099-K Test and Learn Process.

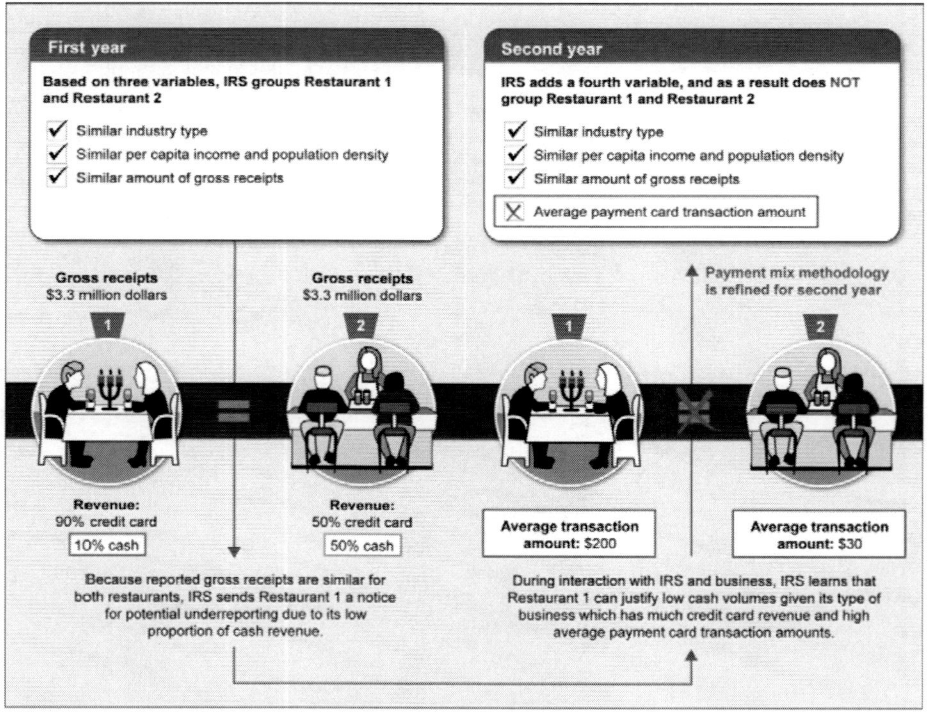

Source: GAO analysis of IRS pilot documentation. | GAO-15-513

Figure 9. Illustration of How IRS Changes the Payment Mix Methodology to Improve Identification of Noncompliant Taxpayers.

In all of the pilot activities, IRS uses taxpayer identification numbers to first match Forms 1099-K with the correct tax returns. IRS then compares Form 1099-K information with business income reported on individual and business tax returns. This process is detailed in figure 8. In the two underreporter pilot activities, IRS compares line by line the gross dollar amount of payments listed on Form 1099-K to gross receipts reported on the tax return to identify potential underreporting of payment card and third-party network revenue.

The payment mix methodology aims to identify potential underreporting of gross receipts from both card and cash sources. For this methodology, IRS first calculates a payment mix—the relative ratio of cash and card revenues of similar businesses. IRS determines this ratio by dividing the gross payment amount on Form 1099-K by gross receipts on the tax return. IRS then computes the amount of potential underreporting by comparing this payment mix to that of similar businesses based on variables including industry type and size, population density, per capita income, and average transaction sizes. As part of the test and learn process, IRS has expanded the number of variables to refine identification of possible underreporting taxpayers. One example of this is illustrated in figure 9.

If implemented successfully and properly evaluated, the payment card pilot could allow IRS to determine which, if any, pilot activities are effective enough to justify broader expansion, including integration with or replacement of other compliance enforcement efforts.

IRS's Evaluation Plan Enabled it to Rapidly Test, Learn from, and Adapt Pilot Activities, but does not Include Key Elements for Assessing Overall Pilot Performance

To assess IRS's plan for evaluating the payment card pilot we used our previously developed guidance to identify key elements for designing quality evaluations.[28] Addressing each element at the overall pilot and pilot activity levels can provide program managers with objective information to iteratively assess program performance. The five key elements we identified for quality evaluation design are described in table 5.

Table 5. Elements of a Program Evaluation Framework

Element	Characteristics
Clarify understanding of the program's goals and strategy.	• Program activities. • Program stages. • Expected short-, medium-, and long-term impact. • Resource investments. • External factors that could affect the outcome.
Develop relevant and useful evaluation questions and an analysis plan.	• Objective and answerable evaluative questions. • Clearly defined criteria.
Assess the relevance and quality of available data sources.	• Description of the information or data and sources needed to assess the program against • the evaluation criteria. • Description of how the information will be gathered. • Description of the tools developed to obtain these data and how they are assessed. • A data reliability assessment.
Address data, scope, and methodology limitations.	• Documentation of assumptions, procedures, and modes of analysis. • Assess that the evaluation fits available time and resources. • Determination that data are free of bias and errors.
Facilitate the use of the evaluation results in program management decision-making.	• Demonstrate leadership support. • Build a strong body of evidence. • Engage stakeholders throughout the evaluation process.

Source: GAO. | GAO-15-513

IRS's evaluation plan for pilot activities integrated many characteristics of a well-designed evaluation. As a result, IRS was able to make rapid, ongoing assessments of pilot activities and continually incorporate changes based on what was learned. This approach allowed IRS to test many hypotheses simultaneously while limiting the number of small business taxpayers affected by the pilot.

However, the overall evaluation plan for the pilot lacked characteristics of each element that are necessary to ensure a quality evaluation. If IRS does not address these gaps, it risks not having the evidence needed to effectively decide whether, how, and when to integrate pilot activities into broader small business compliance improvement efforts.

Clarify Understanding of the Pilot's Goals and Strategy

IRS clearly defined the overall pilot goal, which is to use Form 1099-K data to identify and reduce underreported and unreported income. IRS outlined and detailed the specific program activities it tested and documented pilot planning and results in a strategic planning document and several other executive-level updates. These documents detailed various actions, including internal meetings, assessments, outreach, training, and information technology activities, during the early stages of the pilot. IRS's strategic planning document also provided a conceptual representation of the different stages of the pilot and the growth of compliance case volume at each stage, as seen in figure 10.

IRS has generally documented the expected short-, medium- and long-term impacts of the pilot. One important short-term impact included learning about the small business population to improve identification of noncompliant taxpayers. For example, IRS realized an issue was arising because some small businesses—such as high-end restaurants—have lower cash revenue than other similar businesses. To address this issue, IRS added a line to Form 1099-K to collect data about the number of payment transactions (see figure 11). IRS uses this information to determine the average payment card transaction amount. In the medium term, IRS sees the potential for improved taxpayer voluntary compliance. After the first year of the pilot, IRS tested compliance levels of taxpayers before and after the introduction of the pilot and found that almost half of taxpayers increased their reported gross receipts, and about 60 percent of those contacted reported their income more accurately the following year. In the long term, IRS sees these activities helping to reduce the tax gap.

While IRS has defined high-level pilot goals, such as improving voluntary compliance and reducing the tax gap, it did not establish performance measures for these goals and has not decided on a time frame for developing them. IRS has defined broad stages for pilot implementation, but has not clearly identified measures or indicators to determine when the pilot has moved or will move from one stage to the next.

IRS identified pilot staffing needs. In June 2012, IRS estimated the number of full-time equivalents (FTE) it would need to conduct field exams. IRS officials also said they track resources for some of the pilot activities, including the implementation of the payment mix methodology pilots. However, IRS's evaluation plan has not fully identified and tracked resource needs or use, including the actual numbers of FTEs hired or management resources to design and monitor test and learn pilots.

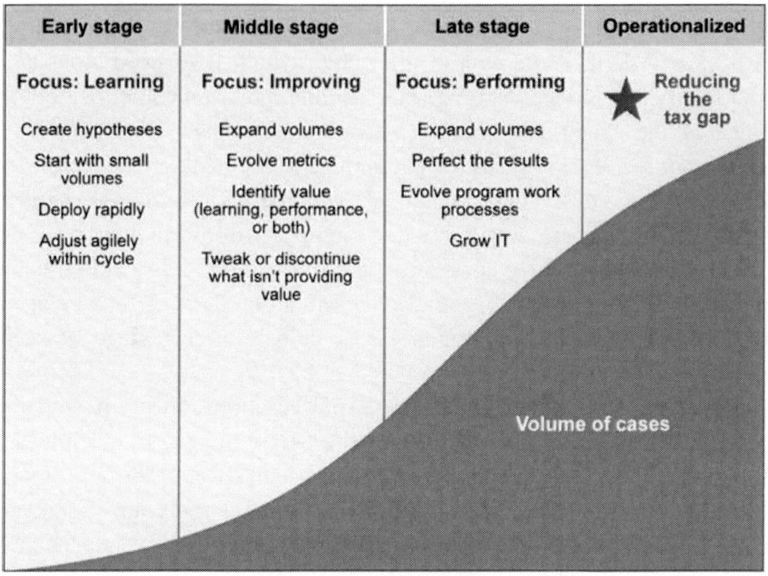

Source: GAO analysis of IRS pilot documentation. | GAO-15-513

Figure 10. IRS's Conceptual Timeline of Pilot Stages.

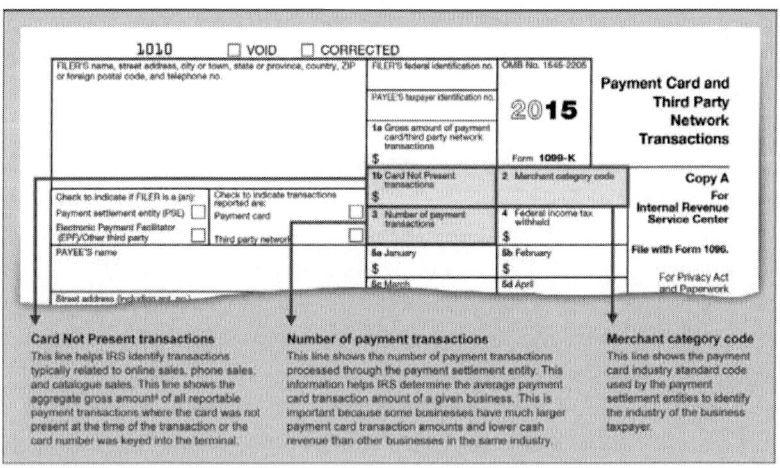

Source: GAO analysis of IRS pilot documentation. | GAO-15-513

[a] The gross amount refers to the total dollar amount of reportable transactions without regard to adjustments including credits, cash equivalents, discount amounts, fees, or refunds.

Figure 11. IRS Changes to Form 1099-K as a Result of Pilot Learning.

IRS identified external factors that could affect the progress or effectiveness of the overall pilot. It identified potential hurdles, including possible litigation and access to necessary technology solutions. However, IRS has not articulated how these factors affect the future of the pilot and what decisions it will make to address them under different scenarios.

Develop Relevant and Useful Evaluation Questions and an Analysis Plan

IRS evaluated pilot activity results, but there is no clear documentation of its evaluation questions or analysis plan. However, these can be inferred based on the evaluation results. According to IRS officials, one of the evaluation goals was to learn why some compliant taxpayers were identified as potential underreporters of income. IRS examined the results of closed cases to learn how to better identify compliant and noncompliant taxpayers. An example of this analysis and resulting change is described in more detail in the text box.

IRS Test and Learn Approach to Improve Identification of Noncompliant Taxpayers

One IRS pilot learning goal is to test a new case selection methodology called the payment mix methodology. IRS is learning how to improve this methodology to better identify noncompliant taxpayers.

When analyzing results of the first year of the pilot program, IRS found that a significant percentage of online-only businesses—which do not accept cash—were falsely identified by the payment mix methodology as potential underreporters of cash income. To decrease the likelihood that compliant online-only businesses were selected in future years, IRS added a line to Form 1099-K that allows the payment settlement entity to specify the aggregate gross amount of all reportable payment transactions during the calendar year where the card was not present at the time of the transaction or the card number was keyed into the terminal. Typically, this relates to online sales, phone sales, or catalogue sales. Because IRS reduces the probability that compliant small business taxpayers are identified as potential underreporters of income, the overall burden for compliant taxpayers is reduced.

Source: GAO analysis of IRS pilot documentation. | GAO-15-513

IRS evaluated the results of all pilot activities. IRS compared the average time to complete an audit and the average dollars assessed in additional tax for each case against existing compliance and enforcement efforts. IRS could use this information to decide which pilot activities to implement in a full compliance program.

IRS did not have evaluative questions and criteria to assess whether the overall pilot or the pilot activities achieved the intended goals or produced the intended results. Understandably, as IRS tests and adapts different approaches, it has learned and will continue to learn which approaches demonstrate the most promise in efficiently and effectively identifying noncompliant taxpayers. Clearly articulated evaluative questions and related analysis plans would allow IRS to determine whether the overall pilot and pilot activities are achieving results that would signal what next steps should be taken. These may include deciding the pilot can move beyond the learning stage, be expanded, or, ultimately, moved from pilot to full implementation as a compliance program. Conversely, the determination could be that the pilot and pilot activities are not achieving the intended results and should be discontinued or modified.

Assess the Relevance and Quality of Available Data Sources

During the early stages of the pilot, part of IRS's evaluation of pilot activities involved assessing Form 1099-K data quality. IRS monitored potential errors that payment settlement entities could make when filling out the form, including invalid or missing taxpayer identification numbers. Such data entry errors could negatively affect IRS's efforts to compare the data with information reported on small business taxpayer returns. When errors were identified IRS contacted the payment settlement entities to make corrections. IRS officials told us that because of this effort, accuracy rates for matching rose from 90.3 percent for tax year 2011 to 95.4 percent for tax year 2013. IRS officials have told us that analysis of Form 1099-K data is ongoing.

Since IRS lacks evaluative questions and an analysis plan for assessing the overall pilot, it does not have complete descriptions of the information or data and sources needed to assess the overall pilot against evaluation criteria, how that information will be gathered, and an assessment of data reliability. Because IRS addressed the relevance and quality of data sources in some of the early evaluations of some pilot activities, this information could feed into the development of the broader evaluation plan.

Address Data, Scope, and Methodology Limitations

IRS documented certain assumptions of its analysis. For example, in the alternative notice pilot, IRS sent assessments to taxpayers who did not respond to the notice and those who admitted to underreporting. IRS referred cases to IRS field work when taxpayers sent insufficient responses or communicated that a review of books and records was necessary.

Furthermore, in the early stages of the pilot, IRS showed evidence that it checked that data were free of errors. In the first year of the pilot, officials took steps to ensure that compliance examiners understood and consistently applied decision rules to determine compliance results.

IRS provided evidence that it estimated timelines and relative resource needs to move from the test and learn phase to a full compliance program. IRS outlined three scenarios to achieve a given level of compliance at program implementation. However, these scenarios were developed without a program level evaluation. Until IRS conducts an evaluation, it will not have the information it needs to determine which approach to take.

Although IRS showed evidence that data, scope, and methodology limitations were considered and addressed for certain pilot activities, these limitations were not fully addressed for the overall pilot. IRS would first need to develop evaluative questions, assessment criteria, and an analysis plan for the overall pilot before it could clearly assess data, scope, and methodology considerations. An assessment of design limitations would include stating any limitations of pilot scope, determining comparisons against which to assess pilot results, and assessing whether the evaluation fits available time and resources. Asking these questions would help clarify the potential impact of any project design limitations when determining whether to move pilot activities toward full program implementation.

Facilitate Use of the Evaluation Results in Program Management Decision Making

IRS provided evidence that leadership from multiple offices across the agency—the Small Business and Self-Employed Division, Office of Compliance Analytics, and the Information Technology Organization—demonstrated commitment to using evaluation data to inform pilot decision making for the beginning of the pilot. Senior officials from each of these offices met weekly during the early stages of the pilot. The leadership actively engaged internal stakeholders and developed strategies to internally communicate information about pilot program activities. These strategies included organizing employee focus groups, training, and leadership updates on pilot progress. For example, in October and November of 2012, IRS provided an update on project communication status to communication directors across all operating divisions.

In addition, IRS leadership engaged with external stakeholders before launching the pilot. In October 2011, IRS addressed small business representatives' concerns about paperwork burdens by announcing that it would not require taxpayers to reconcile gross receipts and merchant card transactions. IRS also worked to address tax practitioner questions about the use of the payment mix methodology for case selection. As a result of the outreach, for example, IRS developed and tested a tool to help tax practitioners determine if their clients would be at risk for underreporting cash transactions.

CONCLUSION

IRS's payment card matching program has the potential to enhance the agency's ability to identify noncompliant small business taxpayers. Better identification of noncompliance would reduce the burden placed on honest taxpayers because the likelihood they would be selected for costly and time-consuming audits or other compliance contacts could be reduced. Further, more effective identification of noncompliant taxpayers means IRS can more efficiently use limited resources.

IRS's Payment Card Pilot shows promise in producing these results. However, IRS has a long road ahead to figure out whether and how the pilot, and its many activities, can be fully implemented. IRS has not clearly defined the stages of the pilot or measurable goals that it can use to determine when the pilot has moved from one stage to the next, or if it should. Without defining the stages and establishing related metrics, IRS will not be able to articulate the pilot's status at critical points in time. Further, it will not be able to justify the investment of additional resources if it cannot demonstrate progress toward those goals. In addition, IRS has not developed a full evaluation plan that will allow for a systematic assessment of the overall pilot against evidence-based criteria. Such a plan is necessary so IRS can ensure that it is making informed decisions about moving forward. Following key elements of evaluation design will help ensure that the results of the evaluation are valid and reliable. Finally, documenting the plan's limitations will reduce the risk that IRS will draw conclusions that are beyond what can be supported.

RECOMMENDATIONS

To improve the evaluation of the payment card pilot, the Commissioner of Internal Revenue should take the following actions:

- Clearly define the stages of the payment card pilot and establish measurable goals for determining when the pilot advances from one stage to the next.
- Develop an evaluation plan for the overall pilot and building on pilot activities to inform decisions about whether, how, and when to integrate pilot activities into overall enforcement efforts. This plan should include
  - evaluation questions,
  - evidence-based evaluative criteria,
  - an analysis plan,
  - a complete description of data to be collected,
  - a data reliability assessment, and
  - documentation of evaluation limitations.

AGENCY COMMENTS

We provided a draft of this report to the Commissioner of Internal Revenue and the Secretary of the Treasury for their review and comment. IRS's Deputy Commissioner for Services and Enforcement provided written comments, which expressed appreciation to GAO for recognizing IRS's efforts to consider taxpayer burden when implementing processes and procedures. In its response to the draft, IRS agreed to incorporate an evidence-based assessment of the payment card pilot that includes identifying clearly defined pilot stages and implementing an evaluation plan with measurable goals. IRS stated it will provide a more detailed response to our recommendations after this report has been released. IRS also provided us with technical comments, which we incorporated into the report as appropriate. Treasury did not provide comments.

James R. McTigue, Jr.
Director, Tax Issues
Strategic Issues

APPENDIX I: OBJECTIVES, SCOPE, AND METHODOLOGY

The objectives of this report are to: (1) describe the characteristics of the small business population; (2) describe how characteristics of a small business affect compliance burden; (3) describe how the Internal Revenue Service (IRS) integrates small business compliance burden considerations in decision making; and (4) assess IRS's plan for evaluating its payment card pilot.

To describe general characteristics of the small business population such as the number of small businesses and total income, we reviewed taxpayer data from IRS Statistics of Income (SOI) and studies with access to taxpayer data. We reviewed SOI documents about data reliability and sampling methodology, and interviewed officials in SOI. We reviewed reports from researchers at the U.S. Department of Treasury, Office of Tax Analysis (OTA). We interviewed two of the OTA authors about their methodology for identifying the small business population. We performed data reliability tests by comparing OTA estimates for all filers against SOI estimates and by comparing OTA estimates for tax year 2007 and 2010. We found the estimates from researchers at OTA were sufficiently reliable for our purposes of describing general characteristics of the small business population. See appendix II for a more detailed discussion of OTA researchers' methodology and assumptions.

To describe how characteristics of a small business affect compliance burden, we conducted a literature review where we reviewed IRS research papers and conference presentations, academic studies, and our prior work on taxpayer compliance burden. We searched relevant databases such as ProQuest, Accounting & Tax, EconLit, ABI/Inform, Nexis.com, and Tax Notes. We identified and reviewed selected IRS studies on tax compliance burden conducted over the last 11 years. We also asked IRS officials from the Research, Analysis, and Statistics (RAS) division to identify any additional IRS research assessing small business tax compliance burden and post-filing burden. To obtain information related to federal small business tax requirements, we reviewed IRS taxpayer guidance found on the IRS website including the 2015 tax calendar. We interviewed relevant IRS officials to clarify our understanding of the research and models, and to verify our analysis.

To describe how IRS integrates small business compliance burden considerations in decision making, we examined IRS's strategic plan and relevant goals and objectives related to taxpayer burden. We also reviewed IRS's Internal Revenue Manual, which outlines, among other things, guiding principles for considering burden reduction. We interviewed IRS officials in the Small Business and Self-Employed division (SB/SE), RAS, and the Office of Taxpayer Burden Reduction about other activities IRS conducts related to taxpayer burden reduction, tools it uses to manage burden reduction efforts, and initiatives it implemented. In addition, we interviewed tax practitioners, associations, and other liaisons to the small business community to identify areas of burden associated with interactions between IRS and the small business community, and discuss what might alleviate burden. We conducted unstructured interviews with a non-generalizable sample of 12 organizations based on their knowledge of small business tax policy resulting from historical involvement and relationships with the small business community and IRS. We reviewed supporting documentation, where available. We selected these organizations to represent a variety of perspectives and groups within the small business community.

To assess IRS's plan for evaluating the payment card pilot, we reviewed and summarized documentation that included IRS's Information Reporting and Document Matching Strategic Roadmap; Communication, Outreach, and Education Strategic Plan; and IRS internal presentations to the IRS Commissioner. We interviewed IRS officials from SB/SE and Office of Compliance Analytics divisions on the pilot to link IRS's test and learn approach to defining strategic goals, evaluation questions, an analysis plan, and the ability to track benefits of the pilot efforts. We compared these efforts to our guidance on program evaluation design and applied criteria adapted from the guidance to both the overall pilot and pilot activities.[29]

We conducted this performance audit from July 2014 to June 2015 in accordance with generally accepted government auditing standards. Those standards require that we plan and perform the audit to obtain sufficient, appropriate evidence to provide a reasonable basis for our findings and conclusions based on our audit objectives. We believe that the evidence obtained provides a reasonable basis for our findings and conclusions based on our audit objectives.

Appendix II: Description of Methodology and Reliability of Data Used to Produce Small Business Population Estimates

For our analysis, we use estimates from researchers at the U.S. Department of the Treasury, Office of Tax Analysis (OTA), to describe the characteristics of the small business population, such as the number of small businesses and total income.[30] There are no universally accepted criteria for defining the small business population. OTA estimates address some of the limitations of describing the small business population using estimates based solely on the type of tax return that is filed by excluding certain tax returns that may not be actual businesses. Not all tax returns that report business income represent business entities with the principal purpose to generate revenue or to engage in substantive business activity. For example, some C corporations can serve as investment vehicles that engage in little or no business activity. Further, partnerships may be created to redistribute profits generated by another partnership and may not generate income themselves.[31] Filers of Form 1040, Schedule C, may be independent contractors who may more closely resemble employees than small businesses. Additionally, rental income for some individuals may be incidental and not represent business activities. Uncertainty within OTA estimates can come from: (1) assumptions that were made to distinguish small businesses engaged in substantial and substantive business activities from other entities that file the same tax return; and (2) that the estimates are based on sampled taxpayer data and subject to sampling error. Consequently, results that are slightly higher or lower than those reported in this particular analysis may be equally valid for describing the numbers of businesses in each subgroup and the size of their incomes. We found the estimates from the researchers at OTA were sufficiently reliable for our purposes of describing general characteristics of the small business population.

Throughout this report, we refer to the estimated number of small business filers as the number of small businesses. Using these estimates may understate the number of small businesses where individual taxpayers can own multiple small businesses. For example, individual taxpayers can file multiple schedules to report business activity (profit, loss, and supplemental income and loss from rental real estate activity) from different lines of business.[32] The number of schedules filed is greater than the number of Form 1040 tax returns to which these schedules are attached due to some returns having multiple schedules.[33] The total income estimates are the sum of all business income reported on tax returns, including gross receipts, rents, dividends, capital gains, royalties, and interest.[34] Total income for Schedule E filers is limited to rental real estate activity from Part I of that schedule to avoid attributing income from pass-through entities or from royalties to these businesses.

The OTA analysis had access to taxpayer data made available by IRS Statistics of Income (SOI).[35] Available data from SOI samples indicate that the sampling errors for the total number of filers and total business receipts for each type of taxpayer is less than +/- 6 percent at the 95 percent confidence level. Sampling errors of subpopulations may be higher where tax returns have been sampled at lower rates. Data were not available to determine sampling errors for the OTA total income measure; however, business receipts make up such a substantial portion of the OTA total income that we would not expect the sampling error to be significantly greater for the OTA total income estimates than it is for the SOI estimates for business receipts. For C corporations, S corporations, partnerships, and sole proprietorships in 2010, the OTA number of filers is within +/- 2 percent of SOI estimates of the number of filers.[36] OTA total income estimates are higher (within + 20 percent) of SOI total receipts estimates for these filers because OTA's total income measure includes types of income other than business receipts.

The estimates used in this report are based on thousands of returns from the 2010 SOI Individual, Corporate, and Partnership Studies. Although we do not know the exact number of records used for each estimate, the Individual sample has 50,464 Form 1040 returns with a Schedule C with a sample selection amount of less than $10 million and 5,804 Form 1040 returns with Schedule F but without a Schedule C. The sample selection amount is the greater of indexed negative income and indexed positive income. The Corporate sample has 20,085 Form 1120 returns with total assets less than $10 million and size of proceeds less than $2.5 million where proceeds is defined as the larger of the absolute value of net income (deficit) or absolute value of cash flow (which includes net income, depreciation, and depletion). The Corporate sample also has 15,741 Form 1120S returns that have total assets less than $10 million and size of proceeds less than $2.5 million. The Partnership sample has 35,744 returns with total assets or current activity measure less than $10 million. Current activity measure is the maximum of the absolute value of receipts and income/loss. In this situation, receipts is the sum of the net receipts, rental income, gross income, portfolio interest income, dividend interest income, royalty income, and net long-term capital gain/loss. Income/loss is the sum of ordinary income, net income, net income from the balance sheet, portfolio interest income, royalty income, and net long- term capital gain/loss.

Table 6 shows SOI estimates for the total number of filers and total income by type of tax return for tax year 2010 (as reported by Prisinzano et al.).[37] The OTA analysis and Prisinzano et al. apply two tests to exclude tax returns filed that do not represent filers that generate substantial income or engage in substantive business activity. The first test is a de minimis activity test that requires taxpayers to report total income or total deductions greater than $10,000, or that their sum be greater than $15,000. The second test requires total deductions be greater than $5,000, which indicates substantive business activity based on expenses related to employees, inventories, and investment, among other things. The application of these two tests results in the exclusion of 46.7 percent of the 44.6 million total tax returns, but only 0.6 percent of the total $33.3 trillion in total income represented by these tax returns.[38]

Table 6. Estimates for the Total Number of Filers and Total Income by Type of Tax Return for Tax Year 2010

	Number of filers (in thousands)	Percent of All Filers	Total income (in billions of dollars)	Percent of Total Income for All Filers
Schedule C Sole Proprietors				
All filers	23,005	100	1,191	100
Small businesses	9,855	42.8	999	83.9
Larger businesses	3	0a	94	7.9
Schedule E-Part I Landlords				
All filers	10,102	100	274	100
Small businesses	4,944	48.9	223	81.4
Larger businesses	0a	0a	5	1.8
Schedule F Farmers				
All filers	2,444	100	154	100
Small businesses	1,451	59.4	144	93.5
Larger businesses	0a	0a	8	5.2
Partnerships				
All filers	3,248	100	5,646	100
Small businesses	2,398	73.8	1,118	19.8

	Number of filers (in thousands)	Percent of All Filers	Total income (in billions of dollars)	Percent of Total Income for All Filers
Larger businesses	70	2.2	4,472	79.2
S corporations				
All filers	4,128	100	5,844	100
Small businesses	3,531	85.6	2,287	39.1
Larger businesses	84	2	3,548	60.7
C corporations				
All filers	1,671	100	20,228	100
Small businesses	1,377	82.4	1,133	5.6
Larger businesses	68	4	19,091	94.4

Source: GAO analysis of data from Richard Prisinzano et al., "Identification of Small Businesses Using Tax Data: 2010 Update," (presented at the 2013 National Tax Association's Spring Symposium, May 17, 2013). | GAO-15-513

Notes: We refer to the estimated number of business and small business filers as the number of businesses and small businesses. The number of individual filers with business income includes taxpayers filing multiple schedules. Small businesses represent tax returns that pass the two tests of the OTA researchers and have $10 million or less in both total income and total deductions. Larger businesses represent tax returns that pass the two tests of the OTA researchers and have more than $10 million in either total income or total deductions. Total income is generally defined as gross receipts, rents, dividends, capital gains, royalties, and interest. Total income for Schedule E filers is limited to rental real estate activity from Part I of that schedule.

[a] These values are rounded and do not equal zero (i.e., the number of filers is less than 500 or the percentage of total filers is less than 0.05 percent for each of these values).

Table 7. Estimates for Total Number of Filers and Total Income by Type of Tax Return for Tax Years 2007, 2010

	Number of filers (in thousands)		Percent change	Total income (in billions of dollars)		Percent change
	2007	2010		2007	2010	
Schedule C Sole Proprietors						
All filers	23,128	23,005	-0.5	1,369	1,191	-13.0
Small businesses	10,669	9,855	-7.6	1,136	999	-12.1

Table 7. (Continued)

	Number of filers (in thousands)		Percent change	Total income (in billions of dollars)		Percent change
	2007	2010		2007	2010	
Schedule E-Part I Landlords						
All filers	9,636	10,102	4.8	253	274	8.3
Small businesses	4,592	4,944	7.7	208	223	7.2
Schedule F Farmers						
All filers	2,510	2,444	-2.6	133	154	15.8
Small businesses	1,468	1,451	-1.1	126	144	14.3
Partnerships						
All filers	3,096	3,248	4.9	6,107	5,646	-7.5
Small businesses	2,219	2,398	8.1	1,175	1,118	-4.9
S corporations						
All filers	3,990	4,128	3.5	6,317	5,844	-7.5
Small businesses	3,460	3,531	2.1	2,424	2,287	-5.7
C corporations						
All filers	1,865	1,671	-10.4	22,089	20,228	-8.4
Small businesses	1,555	1,377	-11.4	1,386	1,133	-18.3

Source: GAO analysis of data from Richard Prisinzano et al., "Identification of Small Businesses Using Tax Data: 2010 Update," (presented at the 2013 National Tax Association's Spring Symposium, May 17, 2013). | GAO-15-513

Note: We refer to the estimated number of small business filers as the number of small businesses. The number of individual filers with business income includes taxpayers filing multiple schedules. Small businesses represent tax returns that pass the two tests of the OTA researchers and have $10 million or less in both total income and total deductions. Total income is generally defined as gross receipts, rents, dividends, capital gains, royalties, and interest. Total income for Schedule E filers is limited to rental real estate activity from Part I of that schedule.

Using this threshold of $10 million or less in both total income and total deductions, small businesses represent 99 percent of tax returns generating substantial income and engaged in substantive business activities (and more than 95 percent of tax returns for each type of tax return). Small businesses account for 17.8 percent of the total income for these tax returns (and more than 91 percent of total income for each type of individual filer and between 5 and 40 percent of total income for each type of corporation and partnership).

Table 7 shows the OTA small business estimates are consistent across the years 2007 and 2010, and are similar to corresponding estimates for all filers. In addition to the measurement errors discussed above, OTA estimates for these tax years are affected by other factors, including changing economic conditions. In spite of these factors, small business estimates for 2010 are within +/- 11 percent of 2007 values for number of filers and within +/- 18 percent of 2007 values for total income. For each type of filer, the percent change from 2007 to 2010 for small businesses is similar to the percent change for all filers (the difference in percent change is within +/- 10 percentage points). We found similar relationships for other subpopulations reported within this report.[39] While we do not have sampling errors for these estimates, we consider estimates of percentages that differ by more than 30 percentage points or totals that differ by more that 100 percent to be different.

Appendix III: Additional Information on Small Business Compliance Burden

The figures and tables in this appendix supplement those in the second objective providing additional information on small business tax-related activities, IRS burden model methodology, and results from IRS burden models.

Table 8 provides a detailed description of tax-related activities that may create burden for small businesses. These activities are grouped by income taxes, employer-related taxes, and third-party information reporting and industry-specific tax activities.

Table 8. Common Sources of Tax Compliance Burden

Income tax activities	
Filing income tax return	File an annual income tax return. Business type determines which form is filed: • Sole proprietors: Form 1040, *U.S. Individual Income Tax Return*, and Schedule C, *Profit or Loss from Business* • C Corporations: Form 1120, *U.S. Corporation Income Tax Return* • S Corporations: Form 1120S, *U.S. Income Tax Return for an S Corporation*, and Schedule K-1, *Shareholder's Share of Income, Deductions, Credits, etc.*

Table 8. (Continued)

Income tax activities	
	• Partnerships: Form 1065, *U.S. Return of Partnership Income*, and Schedule K-1, *Partner's Share of Income, Deductions, Credits, etc.*
Paying income and self employment taxes	Deposit income and estimated self-employment taxes on a quarterly basis. Entity type determines which form is filed: • Sole proprietors: Form 1040-ES, *Estimated Tax for Individuals* • C Corporations: Form 1120-W, *Estimated Tax for Corporations*
	• S Corporations: Form 1120-W, *Estimated Tax for Corporations*, and shareholders file Form1040-ES, *Estimated Tax for Individuals* • Individuals in Partnerships: Form 1040-ES, *Estimated Tax for Individuals*
Employment tax activities	
Withholding and depositing federal employment tax	Withhold and deposit employment tax monthly or semi-weekly. Employment tax liability determines which form is filed: • Report quarterly the amount of personal income tax withheld and Federal Insurance Contributions Act (FICA) paid for each employee on Form 941, *Employer's Quarterly Federal Tax Return.* • Deposit income tax withheld and FICA taxes either monthly or semi-weekly.
Reporting and depositing federal unemployment tax	Report annually and deposit quarterly Federal Unemployment Tax Act (FUTA) tax.
Providing employees with Form W-2	Provide a copy of Form W-2 for calendar year 2014, no later than February 2, 2015.
Reporting and disclosing retirement plan information	Report the following information related to retirement plans annually. Number of employees determines which form is filed: • File Form 5500, *Annual Return/Report of Employee Benefit Plan.* Must be filed electronically. • If a plan has fewer than 100 participants, file Form 5500-SF, *Short Form Annual Return/Report of Small Employee Benefit Plan.* • If there is only one participant, file Form 5500-SF electronically or the paper-only Form 5500-EZ.
Reporting healthcare information	Report information related to health care as determined by number of employees and entity type: • If filing income tax withholding, S corporations are the only entity that must include the valueof health insurance benefits in the wages of S corporation employees who own more than 2% of the S corporation (2% shareholders).

	• Beginning in 2016, employers with 50 or more full-time employees need to file Form 1094-C, *Transmittal of Employer-Provided Health Insurance Offer and Coverage*, and Form 1095-C, *Employer-Provided Health Insurance Offer and Coverage*. Employers must provide a Form 1095-C to each of its full-time employees.
Third-party information reporting and industry-specific tax activities	
Reporting excise tax	Some small businesses report applicable excise taxes, such as environmental taxes, communications taxes, fuel taxes, retail sale of heavy trucks and trailers, luxury taxes on passenger cars, and manufacturers' taxes on a variety of different products. The type of form used depends on the type of small business industry and tax: • File Form 720, *Quarterly Federal Excise Tax Return*, during April, July, October, and January. • File Form 730, *Monthly Tax Return for Wagers*, and pay the tax on wagers accepted during the previous month. • File Form 2290, Heavy *Highway Vehicle Use Tax Return*, and pay the tax annually (or more frequently if vehicles are first used during multiple months of same year).
Reporting miscellaneous income	If required, some small businesses report miscellaneous income. Reporting depends on small business industry number of 1099-MISC forms: • If reporting fewer than 250 1099-MISCs, submit paper forms which are due to IRS by the end of February, along with a Form 1096, *Annual Summary and Transmittal of U.S. Information Returns*. • If reporting 250 or more 1099-MISCs, submit the forms electronically. Electronic submissions due at the end of March can be submitted through IRS's Filing Information Returns Electronically system.
Tax planning and recordkeeping	Tax planning and record keeping are done throughout the year. The complexity of these activities can vary by entity type, number of employees, and total assets. Some of the activities are as follows: • Stay current with changes in tax laws and requirements • Hire a tax professional • Adjust for withholdings • Obtain and organize tax-related records and receipts, including deductible expenses • Monitor the progress of your business • Prepare your financial statements • Prepare your tax returns and support items reported on tax returns

Source: GAO analysis of IRS documents. | GAO-15-513

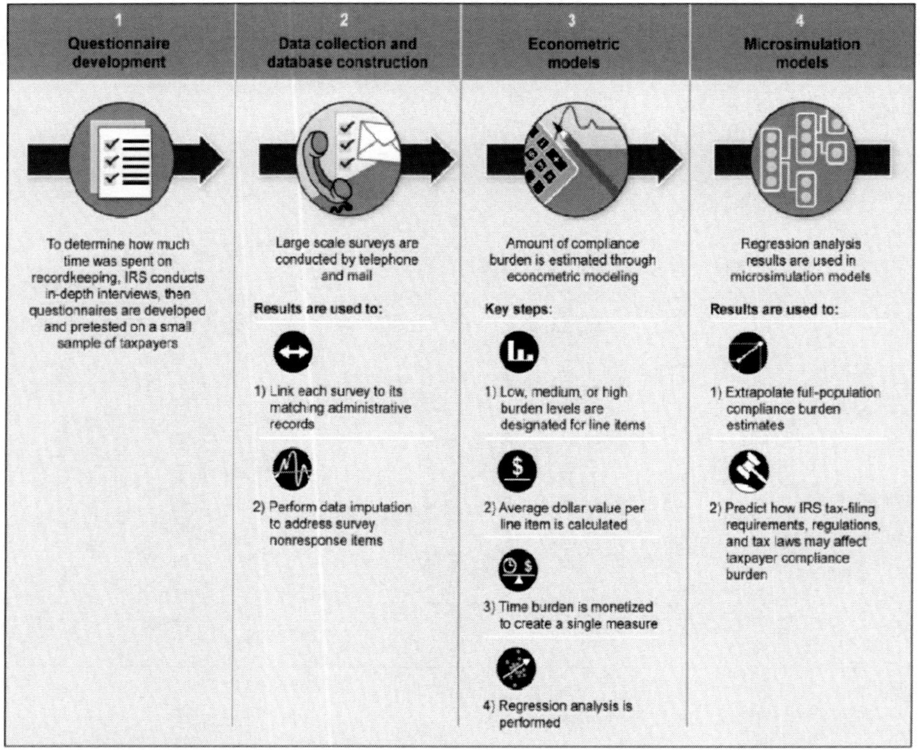

Source: GAO analysis of IRS information. | GAO-15-513

Figure 12. Simplified Depiction of IRS Pre-Filing and Filing Burden Models.

Figure 12 illustrates a simplified depiction of IRS pre-filing and filing burden models. Essentially, IRS uses the data from its compliance burden surveys, combined with data that IRS obtains from the tax returns of survey respondents in econometric models. These models estimate the relationship between taxpayer characteristics and reported burden; the models can then be used to estimate total compliance burden.

IRS then uses estimates of these relationships in simulation models to predict how potential IRS administrative decisions, such as those relating to tax form design and recordkeeping requirements, may affect taxpayer burden. Although such simulation results may provide useful insights, it is difficult to assess the reliability of those results; consequently they should be used with caution.

We found IRS research estimates were reliable for our purposes of obtaining an overview of small business tax compliance costs. One difficulty is that to be able to simulate the effect of burden, IRS needed to develop a complicated methodology for apportioning aggregate burden across all of the different types of pre-filing and filing activities. There are no formal statistical tests to estimate the margins of error around the ultimate simulation results.

The following tables and figure are results from IRS burden models. The data were taken from IRS studies concerning how small business characteristics such as size and industry affect small business compliance costs.

- Tables 9 through 11 examine the estimated pre-filing and filing monetized burden per employee, as a percentage of total receipts, and as a percentage of total assets.
- Table 12 provides information on total monetized business compliance costs by business entity type and total gross receipts across all businesses.
- Table 13 shows the estimated average pre-filing and filing time and money burden by industry.
- Figure 13 provides the estimated post-filing compliance costs for individual filers.

Table 9. Total Monetized Burden per Employee (2002)

	Taxpayers (thousands)		Time and Money Burden (Time monetized at $25/hr)		Time and Money Burden (Time monetized at $40/hr)	
			Per employee		Per employee	
	N	Percentage	Low	High	Low	High
All businesses	7,243	100%	$1,346	$1,458	$1,944	$2,103
Number of employees						
1 to 5	5,680	78.4%	$4,308	$4,746	$6,233	$6,861
6 to 10	662	9.1%	$1,307	$1,365	$1,894	$1,982
11 to 15	310	4.3%	$822	$901	$1,168	$1,271
16 to 25	261	3.6%	$674	$686	$968	$982
26 to 50	204	2.8%	$474	$488	$684	$701
More than 50	126	1.7%	$182	$191	$261	$274

Source: Donald DeLuca et al., "Aggregate Estimates of Small Business Taxpayer Compliance Burden," *IRS Research Bulletin* (2007). | GAO-15-513

Table 10. Total Monetized Burden as a Percentage of Total Receipts (2002)

	Taxpayers (thousands)		Time and Money Burden (Time monetized at $25/hr)		Time and Money Burden (Time monetized at $40/hr)	
			Percentage of receipts		Percentage of receipts	
	N	Percentage	Low	High	Low	High
All businesses	7,243	100%	0.9%	1.0%	1.3%	1.5%
Total receipts						
$0 or less	895	12.4%	n.a.	n.a.	n.a.	n.a.
Less than $10,000	815	11.3%	152.8%	154.5%	216.4%	219.0%
$10,000 to $20,000	303	4.2%	31.6%	32.6%	46.5%	47.5%
$20,000 to $50,000	677	9.3%	17.3%	18.6%	25.4%	26.9%
$50,000 to $100,000	715	9.9%	9.3%	10.9%	13.6%	15.9%
$100,000 to $500,000	2,029	28.0%	3.2%	3.3%	4.6%	4.8%
$500,000 to $1 million	705	9.7%	1.3%	1.4%	1.9%	1.9%
Over $1 million	1,104	15.2%	0.3%	0.3%	0.4%	0.5%

Source: Donald DeLuca et al., "Aggregate Estimates of Small Business Taxpayer Compliance Burden," *IRS Research Bulletin* (2007). | GAO-15-513

Table 11. Total Monetized Burden as a Percentage of Total Assets, by Asset Size (2002)

	Taxpayers (thousands)		Time and Money Burden (Time monetized at $25/hr)		Time and Money Burden (Time monetized at $40/hr)	
			Percentage of assets		Percentage of assets	
	N	Percentage	Low	High	Low	High
All businesses	7,243	100%	1.60%	1.80%	2.4%	2.6%
Total assets						
$0 or less	1,394	19.2%	n.a.	n.a.	n.a.	n.a.
Less than $10,000	872	12.0%	146.6%	178.35%	213.6%	259.1%
$10,000 to $20,000	399	5.5%	38.3%	39.3%	54.4%	55.6%
$20,000 to $50,000	783	10.8%	19.6%	22.2%	28.3%	32.2%
$50,000 to $100,000	780	10.8%	9.8%	10.2%	14.1%	14.5%
$100,000 to $500,000	1,684	23.3%	3.6%	3.7%	5.3%	5.4%
$500,000 to $1 million	515	7.1%	1.3%	1.4%	1.8%	1.9%
Over $1 million	816	11.3%	0.4%	0.5%	0.6%	0.7%

Source: Donald DeLuca et al., "Aggregate Estimates of Small Business Taxpayer Compliance Burden," *IRS Research Bulletin* (2007). | GAO-15-513

Table 12. Business Income Tax Compliance Costs by Size of Receipts, Using a Variable Moderation Rate (2009)

Total Receipts (Millions)	C Corporations	S Corporations	Partnerships	All
Average Compliance Costs ($)				
0 to 0.10	4,700	3,900	6,700	5,300
0.10 to 1	13,000	9,800	18,100	12,500
1 to 10	35,700	27,600	43,500	34,000
10 to 500	157,800	89,800	134,600	128,200
500 and more		504,000	645,800	925,400
All receipt sizes			13,400	11,600

Table 12. (Continued)

Total Receipts (Millions)	C Corporations	S Corporations	Partnerships	All
Total Compliance Costs ($ Billions)				
0 to 0.10	3.7	7.9	14.2	25.9
0.10 to 1	8.8	16.6	14.9	40.3
1 to 10	6.9	9.6	8.7	25.1
10 to 500	4.2	2.2	4.3	10.7
500 and more	1.7	0.0[a]	0.4	2.1
All receipt sizes	25.3	36.3	42.5	104.1

Source: Rosemary Marcuss et al., "Income Taxes and Compliance Costs: How Are they Related?" *National Tax Journal*, vol. 66 no. 4, (December 2013); pp. 833-854. | GAO-15-513

[a] Tax compliance cost is less than $50 million.

Table 13. Estimated Average Small Business Pre-Filing and Filing Time and Money Burden by Industry (2002)

	Taxpayers (thousands)	Average time burden (hours)		Average money burden (dollars)	
		Low	High	Low	High
All business industry	7,243	236	256	$2,068	$2,226
Agriculture, forestry, and fisheries	314	180	184	$ 1,489	$1,590
Mining and Utilities	53	196	210	$1,503	$1,506
Construction	644	311	312	$2,202	$2,558
Manufacturing	323	304	310	$2,740	$2,813
Wholesale trade	334	279	312	$2,306	$2,647
Retail trade	734	325	331	$2,033	$2,208
Transportation and warehousing	163	233	284	$2,371	$2,465
Professional and scientific	1,357	200	206	$2,172	$2,222
Finance, insurance and real estate	1,946	196	219	$2,172	$2,480
Education and health	394	217	220	$2,128	$2,225
Arts and entertainment	798	254	259	$1,453	$1,686
Industry n.e.c[a]	182	180	444	$1,666	$1,674

Source: Donald DeLuca et al., "Aggregate Estimates of Small Business Taxpayer Compliance Burden," *IRS Research Bulletin* (2007). | GAO-15-513

[a] n.e.c. = not elsewhere classified

Case type	Average compliance cost	Median compliance cost	Total number of cases	Total compliance costs
Automated underreporter (AUR)	$230	$90	3,867,000	$889,000,000
Amended	$450	$130	1,168,000	$526,000,000
Collection	$485	$160	5,845,000	$2,835,000,000
Exam: Correspondence	$515	$160	823,000	$424,000,000
Exam: Field	$4,800	$940	137,000	$658,000,000
Exam: Office	$2,165	$470	137,000	$297,000,000
Total	$470	$133	11,977,000	$5,629,000,000

Source: John Guyton and Richard Hodge, “The Compliance Costs of IRS Post-Filing Processes” (paper presented at the Economic and Social Reseacrch Council’s 2014 International Taxation Analysis Conference, January 2014). | GAO-15-513

Figure 13. Estimated Post-Filing Compliance Costs by Originating Function for Individual Filers (2011).

Appendix IV: Selected Open GAO Recommendations to IRS that May Affect Small Business Taxpayer Burden

Benefit to Small Businesses	Open recommendations	Status
Improving telephone service lowers compliance burdens for taxpayers, including small business taxpayers. Better management of IRS risks and resources would benefit all taxpayers, including small businesses that may need and use these services more often.	The Commissioner of the Internal Revenue should direct the appropriate officials to take the following three actions: (1) Systematically and periodically compare its telephone service to the best in business to identify gaps between actual and desired performance. (2) Include specific countermeasures or options in risk management plans that could guide a response when an adverse event occurs. (3) Develop outcomes that are measurable and plans to analyze service changes that allow valid conclusions to be drawn so that information can be conveyed to Congress, IRS management, and others about the effectiveness of IRS's service changes and impact on taxpayers. **Report:** *Tax Filing Season: 2014 Performance Highlights the Need to Better Manage Taxpayer Service and Future Risks*, GAO-15-163 (Washington, D.C.: Dec.16, 2014).	(1) IRS disagreed with this recommendation, noting in February 2015 that it is difficult to identify comparable organizations with a size or scope similar to that of the IRS to identify performance gaps, and that such efforts would not yield improved results over the benchmarking process currently used by IRS. We disagree that IRS's telephone operations cannot be compared to others. We believe this recommendation remains valid and should be implemented. (2) IRS agreed with this recommendation and, in February 2015, reported it has alreadyincluded specific countermeasures or options in risk management plans for those risks ranked highest in likelihood and impact. IRS also reported it considers such efforts to be ongoing as it develops new risk management plans over time. (3) IRS agreed with this recommendation and, in February 2015, reported it is developing outcome measures and plans for analysis to identify and report on the effect of service changes during the 2015 filing season. IRS also reported it anticipates completing this analysis by the end of fiscal year 2015.

Benefit to Small Businesses	Open recommendations	Status
Better focusing IRS's measures, goals, and objectives could increase identification of select noncompliant small businesses and decrease the burden on compliant taxpayers allowing them to better use their scarce resources. Tracking and documenting data can help IRS make better decisions concerning the correspondence audit program. This will help IRS know if the program is efficient and effective. This can also help IRS determine whether its decisions havea disproportionate or negative impact on small businesses.	To reduce the need for taxpayer calls, ensure that IRS is providing taxpayers with more realistic time frames on when IRS will respond, and more efficiently use IRS resources, the Commissioner of the Internal Revenue Service should: (1) Collect data to analyze whether IRS is responding within the time frames cited in the revised audit notices. (2) If IRS delays are continuing, further revise the notices to provide more realistic response times based on the data and take other appropriate actions to ensure efficient use of IRS tax examiner resources. To clarify the desired results of the correspondence audit program and its linkages to IRS-wide activities, the Commissioner of the Internal Revenue Service should: (3) Establish formal program objectives. (4) Ensure that the program measures reflect those objectives. (5) Clearly link those measures with strategic IRS-wide goals on ensuring compliance in a cost-effective way while minimizing taxpayer burden.	According to IRS officials: (1) Correspondence audit program officials analyzed fiscal years 2012-2015 data to provide a monthly breakdown of the volumes of taxpayer correspondence worked in less or more than 75 days. Supporting documentation from IRS is pending. (2) Analysis of fiscal years 2012-2015 data onvolumes of taxpayer correspondence worked in less or more than 75 days led correspondence audit program to conclude they needed to provide taxpayers better information on expected response timeliness by notice and telephone. Officials said they implemented revised automated phone messages in January 2015. Also, program officials decided to change notices to allow individual correspondence audit campuses to enter a customized response date based on their respective inventory levels at the time notices are sent. The notices are expected to be available and implemented in January 2016 after necessary program updates. Supporting documentation from IRS is pending.
Ensuring an effective investment of resources will help IRS identify expected benefits and track whether the benefits were achieved. These	To better inform decisions being made about the correspondence audit program, the Commissioner of the Internal Revenue Service should:	(3) through (5) IRS will review current documentation and ensure there is a clear link establishing the correspondence audit program objectives and measures with the overall IRS

(Continued)

Benefit to Small Businesses	Open recommendations	Status
efforts will help to balance the allocation of resources between providing taxpayers' telephone assistance and reviewing their correspondence. This could be particularly important for small businesses since this taxpayer group may need or use more of IRS's resources.	(6) Document how the decisions are to be made about the correspondence audit program using performance information. (7) Track and use other program data that have not been used to provide more complete performance information, such as taxpayer burden and experience. To better ensure an effective investment of resources in the Correspondence Assessment Program (CEAP) efforts, the Commissioner of the Internal Revenue Service should: (8) Clearly document the intended benefits of ongoing efforts to address identified problems, and the process for measuring and tracking actual benefits. (9) Develop a plan and timeline for implementing the CEAP contractor's recommendations on possible ways to improve the (a) selection of correspondence audit workload and (b) allocation of resources between providing telephone assistance and reviewing taxpayer correspondence. **Report:***IRS Correspondence Audits: Better Management Could Improve Tax Compliance and Reduce Taxpayer Burden*, GAO-14-479 (Washington, D.C.: June 5, 2014).	goals and objectives. Officials also said they will update official guidance as warranted. Actions on these three recommendations are due by March 2016. Supporting documentation on timeframes for specific actions related to these recommendations is pending. (6) IRS will thoroughly document the original plan development process. Action on this recommendation is due by March 2016. Supporting documentation on timeframes for specific actions related to these recommendations is pending. (7) IRS will evaluate the methodology used in several existing studies to determine the mostproductive use of collectability data. Officials also said IRS will evaluate the feasibility of collecting and using additional data. Action onthis recommendation is due by March 2016. Supporting documentation on timeframes for specific actions related to these recommendations is pending. (8) IRS will document the expected benefits of ongoing changes. Action on this recommendation is due by June 2016. Supporting documentation on timeframes for specific actions related to these recommendations is pending.

Benefit to Small Businesses	Open recommendations	Status
		(9) IRS will continue to pursue efforts with research functions to further improve workload selection and maximize resource usage. Action on this recommendation is due by June 2016. Supporting documentation on timeframes for specific actions related to these recommendations is pending.
This could streamline the process for entering installment agreements. These efficiencies could reduce compliance burdens of taxpayers, including small business taxpayers, by decreasing the time it takes IRS to handle installment agreement cases.	The Commissioner of Internal Revenue should develop a set of standardized account entries and eliminate unnecessary redundancy when entering installment agreement data into accounts. **Report:** *2013 Tax Filing Season: IRS Needs to Do More to Address the Growing Imbalance between the Demand for Services and Resources*, GAO-14-133 (Washington, D.C.: Dec. 18, 2013).	IRS agreed that adopting standardized account entries, as we recommended in December 2013, has benefits. However, since the agency changedits installment agreement program, it has decided to evaluate those changes before exploring whether adopting our recommendation will yield increased efficiencies and lower costs without adversely impacting tax administration. IRS officials stated they will provide a status update in October 2015.
This could provide easier access to information and could reduce taxpayer burden, including for small businesses, by enabling examiners to find critical data and documents quicker during the examination.	To increase the effectiveness of IRS's examinations of individual tax returns, the Commissioner of the Internal Revenue Service should: (1) Transcribe data from paper-filed Form 1040 Schedules C and E that are not currently transcribed and make those data available to Small Business and Self-Employed division (SB/SE) examiners for classification. If IRS has evidence that the costs related to transcribing all such data on Schedules C and	As of March 2015, IRS agreed to study: (1) whether to increase data transcription of additional tax return information as GAO recommended in May 2013. The agency also agreed to study whether to use more data from electronically-filed returns. IRS's study is scheduled to be completed by November 2015, and is expected to weigh the benefits tothe agency and the impacts on taxpayers whofile returns electronically.

(Continued)

Benefit to Small Businesses	Open recommendations	Status
	E are prohibitive, IRS could do one or both of the following actions: (a) transcribe less data by transcribing only the missing data for selected line items, such as certain, large expense line items; or (b) develop a budget proposal to fund an initiative for transcribing Schedule C and E. (2) Make all data collected from electronically submitted Form 1040s available to examiners conducting classification. **Report:** *Tax Administration: IRS Could Improve Examinations by Adopting Certain Research Program Practices*, GAO-13-480 (Washington, D.C.: May 24, 2013).	(2) expanding the use of electronic data to enhance return classification while weighing the benefits of increased information against the risks of potential impacts to electronic filing.
Improving telephone and correspondence services, decreasing wait time, and enhancing taxpayer contacts lowers compliance burdens for taxpayers, including small businesses that may need and use these services more often.	The Commissioner of Internal Revenue should: (1) Outline a strategy that defines appropriate levels of telephone and correspondence service and wait time, and lists specific steps to manage service based on an assessment of time frames, demand, capabilities, and resources. (2) Tailor appropriate and timely interventions with taxpayers who file balance due returns by pilot testing risk-based approaches that could include (a)	(1) IRS has taken steps to modify services provided to taxpayers, but has not yet developed a strategy outlining IRS's customerservice goals. (2) IRS agreed with our December 2012 recommendation to pilot more risk-based approaches for contacting taxpayers who have a balance due. However, IRS has reported that because that project was not funded, it used an alternative model to conduct analysis. IRS implemented its updated model in late April

Benefit to Small Businesses	Open recommendations	Status
	implementing the Advanced Consolidated Data Analytics plan, and (b) using more data-driven methods to identify the most appropriate method for contacting a taxpayer. **Report:***2012 Tax Filing: IRS Faces Challenges Providing Service to Taxpayers and Could Collect Balances Due More Effectively*, GAO-13-156 (Washington, D.C.: Dec. 18, 2012).	2014. In October 2014, IRS reported that better (more productive) cases will be assigned to select work streams. Further, in January 2015, IRS officials said they will be placing revised models into production in fiscal year 2015.
This could help IRS better use its resources for examinations that are needed and justified. This would minimize the chances of a compliant small business being subjected to an unnecessary exam.	To help ensure that IRS uses its examination resources efficiently, the Commissioner of the Internal Revenue Service should: (1) Document and analyze the results of examinations involving the Small Employer Health Insurance Tax Credit to identify how much of those results are related to the credit versus other tax issues being examined, what errors are being made in claiming the credit, and when the examinations of the credit are worth the resource investment. (2) Related to the above analysis of examination results on the credit, identify the types of errors with the credit that could be addressed with alternative approaches, such as soft notices. **Report:***Small Employer Health Tax Credit: Factors Contributing to Low Use and Complexity*, GAO-12-549 (Washington, D.C.: May 14, 2012).	(1) As of October 2014, SB/SE analyzed a statistical sample of 2010 examination results for the Small Employer Health Insurance Tax Credit. As a result of the research, SB/SE concluded that the findings do not justify selecting a specific number of returns for examination with the Credit as the primary issue. Instead, they will identify issues as part of the normal classification process, and prepare guidelines for classifiers to reference when selecting returns for examination. (2) As of October 2014, IRS told us that Math Error Authority, fully implemented in January 2014, addresses many of the common errors claiming the Credit. Therefore, there is not an immediate need for alternative approaches, such as soft notices. However, IRS will still consider alternatives.

(Continued)

Benefit to Small Businesses	Open recommendations	Status
Developing metrics, goals, and strategies to plan and gauge progress in enhancing taxpayer assistance can help IRS determine where it could improve service delivery. This could lead to overall taxpayer burden reduction, including for small businesses.	The Commissioner of the Internal Revenue Service should: (1) Develop a new refund timeliness measure and goal to more appropriately reflect current capabilities. (2) Complete an Internet strategy that (a) provides a justification for the implementation of online self-service tools, and includes an assessment of providing online self-service tools that allow taxpayers to access and update elements of their account online; (b) acknowledges the cost and benefits to taxpayers of new online services; (c) sets the time frame for when the online service would be created and available for taxpayer use; and (d) includes a plan to update the strategy periodically. **Report:***2011 Tax Filing: Processing Gains, but Taxpayer Assistance Could Be Enhanced by More Self-Service Tools*, GAO-12-176 (Washington, D.C.: Dec. 15, 2011).	(1) As of October 2014, IRS has yet to develop a new refund timeliness measure. However, IRS has taken steps to identify the number of days it takes to issue a refund in addition to the percentage of refunds receivedin daily increments from 5 to 60 days. (2) IRS has made progress in improving its Internet online services strategy. In September 2012, IRS provided us with an updated version of that strategy. However, IRS still needs to take a number of steps to more fully develop its long-term online strategy. As of February 2015, IRS officials reported that it does not have a separate online services strategy.
Sharing expected release dates for Information Reporting and Document Management (IRDM) regulations and formal guidance will improve implementation of cost basis and transaction settlement reporting.	To improve implementation of cost basis and transaction settlement reporting, the Commissioner of the Internal Revenue Service should: Work with Treasury to share with the public its plans and expected release dates for IRDM	As of June 2014, the IRS web page on information reporting does not provide information on upcoming information guidance, upcoming outreach, or a description of the private letter ruling process. IRS officials said information on letter rulings is

Benefit to Small Businesses	Open recommendations	Status
IRDM's components include aspects of other systems and pilots that administer programs focused on small businesses.	regulations and formal guidance. IRS could consider including information similar to what is posed on the Department of Transportation's or the Financial Industry Regulatory Authority Web sites. IRS should also include other pertinent information regarding IRDM implementation, such as upcoming informal guidance,frequently asked questions, upcoming outreach, and description of the letter ruling process. **Report:***Information Reporting: IRS Could Improve Cost Basis and Transaction Settlement Reporting Implementation*, GAO-11-557 (Washington, D.C.: May 19, 2011).	found elsewhere on www.irs.gov. Regarding coordination with the Department of the Treasury on sharing potential release dates for regulations and formal guidance, IRS did not provide any evidence of this coordination. However, IRS officials said theyshare with external stakeholders the general timeframes for upcoming guidance.
Improving telephone and correspondence services lowers compliance burdens for taxpayers, including small businesses that may need and use these services more often.	To gain efficiencies and improve taxpayer service, the Commissioner of Internal Revenue should direct the appropriate officials to: (1) Determine a customer service telephone standard, and the resources required to achieve this standard based on input from Congress and other stakeholders. (2) Assess business units' needs for holding Contact Analytics calls beyond 45 days and store calls for this period or document that the costs of doing so exceed the benefits. (3) Establish a performance measure for taxpayer correspondence that includes providing timely service to taxpayers.	(1) As of August 2014, IRS's position remained that its measure of telephone service does not need to be revised and the current process for establishing IRS telephone plans is sufficient. However, we continue to believe that a telephone standard would serve as a means of communicating to Congress and others what IRS believes would constitute good service. (2) IRS disagreed with this recommendation. As of August 2014, IRS officials continue to maintain that increasing the recorded call storage beyond 45 days would not be a low cost effort. However, we continue to believe that storing calls for extended periods would

(Continued)

Benefit to Small Businesses	Open recommendations	Status
	Report: *2010 Tax Filing Season: IRS's Performance Improved in Some Key Areas, but Efficiency Gains Are Possible in Others*, GAO-11-111 (Washington, D.C.: Dec. 16, 2010).	allow IRS to better identify trends and taxpayer concerns, thus offsetting the costs. (3) IRS agreed with this recommendation andstarted using more detailed performance measures that includes an overaged/timeliness measure for its correspondence beginning in fiscal year 2011. However, in April 2014, we reported that overaged correspondence increased from 25 to 47 percent; thus, we continue to believe that elevating this measure to IRS's suite of balanced measures would help provide more visibility and ultimately better service.
(1) It will allow IRS to develop a cost-effective strategy to identify payers that never submit 1099-MISCs. This could alleviate the burden on compliant taxpayers, including small businesses. (2) By knowing more about these characteristics IRS can develop more effective strategies to increase 1099-MISC submissions. This could also alleviate the burden on compliant taxpayers, including small businesses.	To gauge the extent of 1099-MISC payer noncompliance and its contribution to the tax gap, we recommend that the Commissioner of the Internal Revenue Service, as part of future research studies: (1) Develop an estimate of 1099-MISC payer noncompliance. (2) Determine the nature and characteristics of those payers that do not comply with 1099-MISC reporting requirements so that this information can be factored into an IRS-wide strategy for increasing 1099-MISC payer compliance.	(1) According to IRS, developing such an estimate requires a multi-pronged approach and a large amount of coordinated effort. As of September 2014, IRS estimates results willbe available in December 2015. (2) IRS researchers are collecting data on 1099-MISC reporting as part of its National Research Program study on employment taxes, a program that involves examinations of a sample of tax returns expected to culminate in 2015. As of September 2014, IRS estimates results will be available in December 2015.

Benefit to Small Businesses	Open recommendations	Status
	Report: *Tax Gap: IRS Could Do More to Promote Compliance by Third Parties with Miscellaneous Income Reporting Requirements*, GAO-09-238 (Washington, D.C.: Jan. 28, 2009).	

Source: GAO analysis of prior reports. | GAO-15-513

End Notes

[1] U.S. Census Bureau, *Statistics of U.S. Businesses: Employment and Payroll Summary: 2012* (February 2015).

[2] GAO, *Tax Gap: Sources of Noncompliance and Strategies to Reduce It*, GAO-12-651T (Washington, D.C.: Apr. 19, 2012).

[3] 26 U.S.C. § 6050W; 26 C.F.R. §§ 1.6050W-1, 1.6050W-2.

All of a merchant's payment card transactions are reportable on Form 1099-K. However, third-party network transactions are only reportable if a merchant's aggregate amount of such payments for the year exceeds $20,000 and if the aggregate number of transactions exceeds 200.

[4] Appendixes I and II include more detailed information on the scope, methodology, and research analyzed for the first objective.

[5] Criteria were developed from GAO, *Program Evaluation: Strategies to Facilitate Agencies' Use of Evaluation in Program Management and Policy Making*, GAO-13-570 (Washington, D.C.: June 26, 2013), and *Designing Evaluations: 2012 Revision*, GAO-12-208G (Washington, D.C.: January 2012).

[6] GAO, *Tax Policy: Differences in Definitions and Rules in the Tax Code*, GAO-14-652R (Washington, D.C.: July 18, 2014).

[7] GAO, *Partnerships and S Corporations: IRS Needs to Improve Information to Address Tax Noncompliance*, GAO-14-453 (Washington, D.C.: May 14, 2014).

[8] The IRS models we reviewed for this report focus only on federal tax obligations.

[9] IRS and our past reports have used the terms compliance costs and compliance burden interchangeably.

[10] We use estimates from OTA researchers to describe the characteristics of the small business population. We refer to the estimated number of small business filers as the number of small businesses. See Richard Prisinzano, Jason DeBacker, John Kitchen, Matthew Knittel, Susan Nelson, and James Pearce, "Identification of Small Businesses Using Tax Data: 2010 Update" (presented at the 2013 National Tax Association's Spring Symposium, May 17, 2013); Office of Tax Analysis, Department of the Treasury, Matthew Knittel, Susan Nelson, Jason DeBacker, John Kitchen, James Pearce, and Richard Prisinzano, *Methodology to Identify Small Businesses and Their Owners*, Technical Paper 4 (August 2011); and appendix II for further discussion of the data.

[11] The OTA total income measure serves as a proxy for the total business activity, and is not the same as taxable income. In particular, costs of doing business are not deducted and business losses are not used to offset other types of income.

[12] Researchers at OTA define a taxpayer as engaging in substantial and substantive business activity if (1) total income or deductions exceed $10,000, or their sum exceeds $15,000; and (2) total deductions exceed $5,000. These two tests help indicate whether the entity generates non-negligible income and if the entity behaves as a business, respectively.

[13] Researchers at OTA define small businesses as employers if labor deductions are greater than $10,000. Schedule E-Part I landlords are categorized as non-employers because those returns lacked the necessary information to determine labor expenses for these businesses. While Schedule C sole proprietors report contract labor (line 11, Schedule C) and Schedule F farmers report labor hired (line 22, Schedule F), there is no equivalent information reported on Schedule E-Part I.

[14] We are not presenting a comprehensive list of all tax-related activities. Rather, we are highlighting some of the more common activities to provide a general sense of the range of activities small business taxpayers conduct to comply with tax laws.

[15] 44 U.S.C. §§ 3501–3520. For additional information on IRS methodologies see the following studies: Donald DeLuca, John Guyton, Wu-Lang Lee, John O'Hare, and Scott Stilmar, "Aggregate Estimates of Small Business Taxpayer Compliance Burden," *IRS Research*

Bulletin (2007) pp. 147-184; Arnold Greenland, Erica Layne Morrison, David Connors, John L. Guyton, and Michael Sebastiani, "IRS Post-filing Processes Simulation Modeling: A Comparison of DES With Econometric Microsimulation in Tax Administration," *Proceedings of the 2007 Winter Simulation Conference* (IEEE, 2007) pp. 1268-1274; Donald DeLuca, Arnie Greenland, John Guyton, Sean Hennessy, and Audrey Kindlon, "Measuring the Tax Compliance Burden of Small Businesses," *IRS Research Bulletin* (2005) pp. 75-95; Donald DeLuca, Arnold Greenland, Sean Hennessy, Audrey Kindlon, and Michael Stavrianos, "The Tax Compliance Burden of Small Businesses-A Profile of 50 Businesses," *IRS Research Bulletin* (2004) pp. 97-137.

[16] See appendix III, figure 12 for a more detailed discussion of IRS models.

[17] Donald DeLuca et al., "Aggregate Estimates of Small Business Taxpayer Compliance Burden."

[18] IRS reported aggregate estimates for the total small business population using sample weights. To address extreme outlier values, IRS reported ranges in burden estimates to account for any potential bias due to response errors. The low end of the range reflects treating outliers as missing and imputing responses. The high end of the range reflects an approach that caps the extreme values at five standard deviations from the mean for the responses.

[19] These results are presented in Rosemary Marcuss, et.al., "Income Taxes and Compliance Costs: How Are they Related?", *National Tax Journal*, December 2013, 66 (4), pp. 833-854 and George Contos, et.al., "Taxpayer Compliance Costs for Small Businesses: Evidence from Corporations, Partnerships, and Sole Proprietorships," (2009) *Proceedings of the One Hundred Second Annual Conference on Taxation* pp. 50-59, National Tax Association, Washington, D.C.

[20] GAO, Tax Administration: *Costs and Uses of Third Party Information Returns*, GAO-08-266 (Washington, D.C.: Nov. 20, 2007).

[21] GAO, *Small Business: Taxpayers Face Many Layers of Requirements,* GAO/T-GGD-99-76 (Washington, D.C.: Apr. 12, 1999).

[22] IRS, *Strategic Plan: FY2014-2017* (Washington, D.C.: 2014).

[23] IRS, *Internal Revenue Service: Management's Discussion and Analysis, Fiscal Year 2014* (Washington, D.C.: 2014).

[24] See appendix I for a more detailed description of our interviews.

[25] GAO, *Tax Filing Season: 2014 Performance Highlights the Need to Better Manage Taxpayer Service and Future Risks,* GAO-15-163 (Washington, D.C.: Dec. 16, 2014).

[26] The employer mandate is a requirement that all businesses with 50 or more full-time equivalent employees (FTE) provide qualifying health insurance to 95 percent of their full- time employees, or pay a tax penalty if one full-time employee receives the premium tax credit. 26 U.S.C. § 4980H. The employer mandate itself was delayed, in part, to reduce compliance burden. Despite that delay, IRS guidance was still finalized later than initially planned, which representatives said created additional burden.

[27] 26 U.S.C. § 6050W; 26 C.F.R. §§ 1.6050W-1, 1.6050W-2. Section 6050W requires payment settlement entities to provide IRS with merchants' tax identification number and tax filing name. There are two types of payment settlement entities: merchant acquiring entities, such as credit card companies, and third-party settlement organizations, such as PayPal and certain toll road providers. Unlike payment card transactions, third-party network transactions are only reportable if a merchant's aggregate amount of such payments for the year exceeds $20,000 and if the aggregate number of transactions exceeds 200.

[28] Criteria were developed from GAO, *Program Evaluation: Strategies to Facilitate Agencies' Use of Evaluation in Program Management and Policy Making*, GAO-13-570 (Washington, D.C.: June 26, 2013), and *Designing Evaluations: 2012 Revision*, GAO-12-208G (Washington, D.C.: January 2012).

[29] Criteria were developed from GAO, *Program Evaluation: Strategies to Facilitate Agencies' Use of Evaluation in Program Management and Policy Making*, GAO-13-570 (Washington, D.C.: June 26, 2013), and *Designing Evaluations: 2012 Revision*, GAO-12-208G (Washington, D.C.: January 2012).

[30] We use estimates from OTA researchers to describe the characteristics of the small business population. We refer to the estimated number of small business filers as the number of small businesses. See Richard Prisinzano, Jason DeBacker, John Kitchen, Matthew Knittel, Susan Nelson, and James Pearce, "Identification of Small Businesses Using Tax Data: 2010 Update" (presented at the 2013 National Tax Association's Spring Symposium, May 17, 2013); Office of Tax Analysis, Department of the Treasury, Matthew Knittel, Susan Nelson, Jason DeBacker, John Kitchen, James Pearce, and Richard Prisinzano, *Methodology to Identify Small Businesses and Their Owners*, Technical Paper 4 (August 2011).

[31] GAO, *Partnerships and S Corporations: IRS Needs to Improve Information to Address Tax Noncompliance*, GAO-14-453 (Washington, D.C.: May 14, 2014).

[32] This information is filed on the following forms: Schedules C (Form 1040), *Profit or Loss From Business*; Schedule E-Part I (Form 1040), *Supplemental Income and Loss,* with rental real estate activity; and Schedule F (Form 1040), *Profit or Loss From Farming*.

[33] An alternative approach to estimating the number of small businesses is to treat each schedule attached to Form 1040 returns as a separate business. This alternative approach could help inform about the unique burdens associated with filing specific schedules. For an example that takes a similar approach, see Edith Brashares, Matthew Knittel, Gerald Silverstein, and Alexander Yusavage, "Calculating the Optimal Small Business Exemption Threshold for a U.S. VAT," *National Tax Journal*, vol. 67, no. 2 (June 2014): 283–320. Comparing the methodologies from Brashares et al. and Prisinzano et al. applied to filers of Form 1040 Schedule C in tax year 2007, the number of qualifying Schedules C filed is 25.5 million compared to 23.1 million total taxpayers filing at least one Schedule C.

[34] This total income measure serves as a proxy for total business activity and is not the same as taxable income. In particular, costs of doing business are not deducted and business losses are not used to offset other types of income.

[35] OTA researchers developed estimates from tax return data from SOI samples and applying minimal business activity tests and other methodologies to identify unique business entities. The methodologies and assumptions used in this research are important to consider when interpreting these data.

[36] The OTA data for Schedule E renters differs from estimates in SOI publicly published data tables due to OTA's limitation to only individuals with rental real estate activity on Schedule E, Part I. The OTA data for Schedule F farmers differs from SOI estimates due to the inclusion of individuals filing Form 4835 in addition to those filing Schedules F.

[37] Access to SOI micro-level data allows researchers to identify populations based on characteristics of tax returns and to create unique measures of income. This results in studies with access to SOI micro-level data reporting different values for the same taxpayer types. For example, Prisinzano et al. defines the population of Form 1040, Schedule E-Part I landlords using tax returns that report rental real estate activity on Part I. Publicly available SOI data tables estimate the number Form 1040 filers with income from either rent or royalties. Despite the different approach to identify taxpayers with rental income, the 2010 Prisinzano et al. estimate is within -6 percent of the SOI estimate. In contrast, the Prisinzano et al. estimate of Form 1040, Schedule F farmers includes tax returns of farm land owners that file Form 4835, *Farm Rental Income and Expenses*. The resulting estimate is within +25 percent of the SOI estimate of Form 1040 tax returns with Schedule F. The Prisinzano et al. estimates for the number of S corporations, partnerships, and sole proprietorships are the same as SOI estimates, while the estimate for the number of C corporations is within 2 percent of the SOI estimate.

[38] The inherent risk of setting these thresholds is that some of the tax returns excluded from the data may be small businesses of interest when considering tax compliance burdens. Without access to taxpayer data we cannot assess the efficacy of the de minimis test and test for substantive business activities. OTA researchers said they performed sensitivity tests based on different definitions of small businesses, which did not impact their Findings.

[39] For each type of filer and for both number of filers and total income, the difference in percent change from 2007 and 2010 for businesses and for all filers is within +/- 7 percentage points. These differences in percent change for small business employers and all filers are each within +/- 12 percentage points.

In: Small Business Tax Compliance
Editor: Sheri Patton
ISBN: 978-1-63484-565-6

Chapter 2

OPENING STATEMENT OF STEVE CHABOT, CHAIRMAN, HOUSE COMMITTEE ON SMALL BUSINESS. HEARING ON "HOW TAX COMPLIANCE OBLIGATIONS HINDER SMALL BUSINESS GROWTH"*

Good morning. Thank you all for being here. A special thanks to our witnesses who have taken time away from their undoubtedly busy schedules to be with us.

Earlier this year, our committee heard from a man named Scott, who owns a small mattress factory in Franklin, Ohio. Scott *wants* to pay his taxes – he probably wishes he could pay less, but more than anything he wishes it could be simpler. He wants a flatter and fairer code that is more predictable.

Scott is emblematic of the small business community. There are millions of Americans out there just like Scott, who feel the weight of the tax code each day. I speak to them every time I am back home. And I hear the same concerns again and again: more Americans are frustrated with the *process* of paying their taxes than with *actually writing the check to the government. It's unacceptable and we must do better by these people.*

Making the tax code simpler is particularly important for American small business owners, as they are disproportionately affected by tax complexity – a finding that unfortunately, has not changed with time. Studies conducted by

---

* This is an edited, reformatted and augmented version of a statement presented July 22, 2015 before the House Committee on Small Business.

Office of Advocacy at the SBA over the past 10 years found that small firms pay 67% more to comply with the tax code than large firms do. A recent update to those Advocacy studies found that firms with less than 50 employees pay, on average, $1,518 per employee in tax compliance costs, whereas firms with more than 100 pay $647.

It is because of statistics like that why, in 2013, this committee requested that the Government Accountability Office examine the dynamics of small firms and their tax compliance burden. I would like to point out that right at the end of the report the GAO outlines 25 separate recommendations that they have made to the IRS over the past few years that could (and probably would, in my estimation) help reduce taxpayer compliance burdens. The IRS has implemented none of them. And that is a problem.

To be fair, I am not blaming only the IRS for this problem. Congress has been just as guilty. The tax code has grown to nearly 74,000 pages. The IRS did not do that; Washington did.

This committee is and will continue listening to the American people and working with them to make the tax code simpler and less stressful. Again, I want to thank each of our witnesses for taking the time to be with us today.

In: Small Business Tax Compliance
Editor: Sheri Patton
ISBN: 978-1-63484-565-6

Chapter 3

STATEMENT OF TROY LEWIS, VICE PRESIDENT, HERITAGE BANK. HEARING ON "HOW TAX COMPLIANCE OBLIGATIONS HINDER SMALL BUSINESS GROWTH"*

INTRODUCTION

Chairman Chabot, Ranking Member Velazquez, and Members of the House Committee on Small Business, thank you for the opportunity to testify today on "How Tax Compliance Obligations Hinder Small Business Growth." My name is Troy Lewis. I am the vice president and chief enterprise risk management officer at Heritage Bank in St. George, Utah. I am also a sole tax practitioner, adjunct faculty member at Brigham Young University and Chair of the Tax Executive Committee of the American Institute of Certified Public Accountants (AICPA). I am pleased to testify today on behalf of the AICPA.

The AICPA is the world's largest member association representing the accounting profession, with more than 400,000 members in 145 countries and a history of serving the public interest since 1877. Our members advise clients on federal, state and international tax matters, and prepare income and other tax returns for millions of Americans. Our members provide services to

---

* This is an edited, reformatted and augmented version of a statement presented July 22, 2015 before the House Committee on Small Business.

individuals, not-for-profit organizations, small and medium-sized business, as well as America's largest businesses.

The AICPA applauds the leadership taken by the Committee to consider ways to reduce the complexity faced by small businesses when preparing their taxes. Small businesses are the foundation of the U.S. economy, employing over half of the private-sector workforce and creating nearly two-thirds of this nation's net new jobs over the past decade and a half.[1]

Unfortunately, compliance with federal tax laws can act as a road block in the growth of small business. Unlike large multi-national corporations, the time spent by small businesses in complying with tax laws is much more costly because small businesses do not have the luxury of critical mass and a large customer base with which to efficiently spread non-value added compliance costs. Time devoted to complying with tax laws has an impact on business creation, job growth and economic prosperity of these small businesses.

At the same time, we recognize that tax compliance is necessary. However, to help small businesses grow, Congress and the Internal Revenue Service (IRS) should seek to lessen these compliance burdens on all small businesses. When evaluating whether or not a tax compliance requirement should be mandated for a small business, a cost/benefit analysis should first be considered. Nowhere is it more important to ask if the end result is worth the effort than in the area of tax compliance for small businesses.

Using this cost/benefit approach, may I suggest a few areas where Congress can act to reduce the burden of tax compliance in a way that allows small businesses to grow without creating undue hindrances.

IRS TAXPAYER SERVICES

It is imperative that small businesses and their tax return preparers have the ability to communicate with the IRS when preparing their taxes and addressing compliance issues. However, there has been increasingly limited access to the agency and, as reported by IRS Commissioner John Koskinen, "abysmal" level of taxpayer service this year.[2]

Our members have expressed their deep concerns regarding their ability to effectively represent small businesses and other taxpayers in an environment where the IRS service levels are so degraded that:

- During the 2015 tax season, the IRS answered only 37% of the telephone calls received from taxpayers seeking to speak with an assistor;[3]
- The average hold time for the Practitioner Priority Service telephone line reached 47 minutes;[4] and
- According to the National Taxpayer Advocate, the IRS's ability to process taxpayer correspondence in a timely manner declined by 16% since 2014, leaving a backlog of almost 79,000 cases.[5]

Through an informal membership survey we conducted earlier this year, we learned that over half of our members were either somewhat dissatisfied or very dissatisfied with the services they received from the IRS this filing season. This is no surprise considering that only 17% of our members responded that the IRS generally answered their telephone calls within 30 minutes. Most of our members were on hold for extended periods of time and other members noted that they generally had to end their own calls because they did not have the time to wait on hold for an IRS agent to answer.

As reported by one of our members, "I was on hold for over an hour and a half. When the IRS agent finally picked up the call, they needed to transfer to another agent. I had to wait on hold for another hour. Finally, I received a recorded message that the office was closed and I needed to call again the following day."

Many of our members also experienced what the IRS refers to as "courtesy disconnects." According to the IRS, they terminate telephone calls from small businesses and other callers, without taking a message or getting contact information, if the caller has been on hold for two hours. As of April 18th this year, approximately 8.8 million calls received by the IRS were subject to their "courtesy disconnect" policy, which represents an increase from approximately 544,000 over last year.[6] Nothing is more discouraging, frustrating or inefficient for a caller (whether they are a small business or a tax preparer calling on behalf of a small business) than being hung up on by the IRS after waiting on hold for two hours.

Our survey also indicated similar, unacceptable patterns with regards to delays in written correspondence. On average over half of the correspondence sent to the IRS is not responded to within 90 days of receipt.[7] Often small businesses are anxiously awaiting a response to a notice. Furthermore, the longer the response time by the IRS, the more interest and penalties are accrued as the small business attempts to resolve their issue.

We appreciate and understand that the IRS has new initiatives and vital unmet obligations and responsibilities (such as addressing identity theft), but taxpayer service must remain a high priority in order for small businesses to receive the assistance they need on tax issues.

GOOD TAX POLICY

In order to reduce the overall tax compliance burden on small businesses, the AICPA urges the Committee to consider comprehensive tax reform that focuses on simplification, transparency and other *Principles of Good Tax Policy.*[8] We believe it is important to promote a tax system that is perceived as balanced, fair to all, administrable, economically efficient, transparent, and neutral in its effect on economic activity.

Our current tax system is heavily burdened by complexity. Multiple and duplicative tax calculations, definitions, and preferences lead to taxpayer confusion and, thus, errors and frustration. Attempts to adjust tax liabilities through special rules affecting taxable income rather than the rate schedule add to complexity. Business provisions that require retention of records solely for tax purposes increase compliance costs. We urge consideration of removing duplicative rules and definitions, and reducing recordkeeping and calculations, to achieve simplicity, without adding new complexities.

It is also important for an effective tax system and informed citizenry that taxpayers understand the tax system and how it affects them. Clarity of the tax consequences of taxpayers' regular activities is a must. Transparency also helps improve voluntary compliance.

Additionally, it is critical for taxpayers to have certainty to perform any long-term tax planning. Permanence of tax provisions can have substantial impacts on the growth of small businesses. The uncertainty of tax legislation creates unnecessary confusion, anxiety and administrative financial burdens. Without permanency in the Internal Revenue Code ("Code"), we are concerned about the following consequences:

- Impact on a company's financial accounting and reporting;
- Complexity and administrative burden for taxpayers and the IRS;
- Adverse impact on small businesses and ultimately jobs and growth;
- Effect on economic decisions and tax payments; and

- Lack of transparency and certainty with short-term, retroactive extensions

We recognize that it is not always possible for each tax provision and the overall tax system to equally meet each of the ten principles of good tax policy. However, it is important to carefully balance these principles to achieve a respected and administrable tax system.

Tangible Property Regulations

A challenging tax compliance burden that small businesses had to deal with this year was the new final tangible property regulations (TD 9636). These tax rules, which address how businesses should report the acquisition and improvement of tangible property, comprise almost 500 pages of technical guidance and procedures.

While we appreciated that the regulations clarified some rules and provided several small business favorable provisions, we were concerned that they were significantly burdensome for many small business taxpayers because of the required retrospective analysis and reporting requirements.

The AICPA pushed hard for relief and stressed that time was of the essence as a significant portion of the burdens placed on small businesses (and their tax practitioners) would occur prior to filing season. However, despite these pleadings, the IRS issued the much-needed relief, Rev. Proc. 2015-20, on February 13, well into the filing season. Unfortunately, some small businesses and their tax practitioners had already spent time and resources attempting to comply with the new regulations prior to the IRS's issuance of relief. If the IRS had acted in a timely manner, small businesses could have been spared some administrative burden.

Currently, small businesses must prove that expensing such amounts "clearly reflects income" to deduct amounts higher than the $500 threshold. The clear reflection of income test can be challenging for any taxpayer, especially for small businesses. The test is based on the taxpayer's facts, circumstances, and interpretations of those facts and circumstances by the taxpayer and IRS. Thus, it is arbitrary and often difficult to apply. Large businesses (e.g., taxpayers with an AFS), however, are allowed the higher $5,000 threshold. Subjecting small businesses to the clear reflection of income test at merely $500, adds unnecessary complexity and compliance burdens to small businesses.

There are other issues that remain open in regards to the repair regulations. The AICPA recommends that you take immediate action to increase the $500 de *minimis* safe harbor threshold for taxpayers without an AFS to $2,500, and provide for annual adjustments for inflation, to offer meaningful relief to small business taxpayers. To further reduce administrative burden on these rules, we also recommend that you expand the AFS definition to include a reviewed set of financial statements[9] to permit more business to benefit from the higher $5,000 de *minimis* safe harbor threshold.

CIVIL TAX PENALTIES

An additional concern[10] for small businesses is the numerous unfair or untargeted penalty provisions in the Code pertaining to tax compliance. Penalties should deter bad conduct without deterring good conduct or punishing small businesses which are acting in good faith.

Targeted, proportionate penalties that clearly articulate standards of behavior and that are administered in an even-handed and reasonable manner encourage voluntary compliance with the tax laws. On the other hand, overbroad, vaguely-defined, and disproportionate penalties, particularly those administered as part of a system that automatically imposes penalties or that otherwise fail to provide basic due process safeguards, create an atmosphere of arbitrariness and unfairness that is likely to discourage voluntary compliance.

For example, penalties should apply prospectively to future conduct and not retroactively to conduct that was appropriate at the time the conduct occurred. Good tax policy would also suggest that we avoid strict liability provisions that do not grant the IRS discretion to take into consideration the facts and circumstances of a particular business' situation.

The AICPA points out the following specific penalty-related issues with the current system below.

Repeal Technical Termination Rule

The AICPA recommends a repeal of section 708(b)(1)(B) regarding the technical termination of a partnership as it is a trap for the unwary.[11] Under current law, when a partnership is technically terminated, the legal entity continues, but for tax purposes, the partnership is treated as a newly formed entity. The current law requires the partnership to select new accounting methods and periods, restart depreciation lives, and make other adjustments. Furthermore, under the current law, the final tax return of the "old" partnership is due the 15th day of the fourth month after the month-end in which the partnership underwent a technical termination.[12]

A technical termination most often occurs when, during a 12-month period there is a sale or exchange of 50% or more of the total interest in partnership capital and profits. Because this 12-month time frame can span a year-end, the partnership may not realize that a 30% change (a minority interest) in one year followed by a 25% change in another year, but within 12 months of the first, has caused the partnership to terminate.

In practice, this earlier required filing of the old partnership's tax return often goes unnoticed because the company is unaware of the accelerated deadline due to of the equity transfer. Penalties are often assessed upon the business as a result of the missed deadline. Although ignorance is not an acceptable excuse, this technical termination area is often misunderstood and misapplied. The acceleration of the filing of the tax return, to reset depreciation lives and to select new accounting methods, serves little purpose in terms of abuse prevention and serves more as a trap for the unwary.

Late Filing Penalties

Sections 6698 and 6699 impose a penalty of $195 per partner related to late-filed partnership or S corporation returns. The penalty is imposed monthly not to exceed 12 months, unless it is shown that the late filing is due to reasonable cause.

The AICPA proposes that a partnership (or S Corporation), comprised of 50 or fewer partners/shareholders, each of whom are natural persons (who are not nonresident aliens), an estate of a deceased partner, a trust established under a will or a trust that becomes irrevocable when the grantor dies, and domestic C corporations, will be considered to have met the reasonable cause test and will not be subject to the penalty imposed by section 6698 or 6699 if:

- The delinquency is not considered willful under section 7423;
- All entity income, deductions and credits are allocated to each owner; and
- Each partner/shareholder fully reported its share of income, deductions and credits of the entity on its timely filed federal income tax return.

Failure to Disclose Reportable Transactions

Taxpayers who fail to disclose a reportable transaction are subject to a penalty under section 6707A of the Code. For penalties assessed after 2006, the amount of the penalty is 75% of the decrease in tax shown on the return as a result of the transaction (or the decrease that would have been the result if the transaction had been respected for federal tax purposes). If the transaction is a listed transaction (or substantially similar to a listed transaction), the maximum penalty is $100,000 for individuals and $200,000 for all other taxpayers. In the case of reportable transactions other than listed transactions, the maximum penalty is $10,000 for individuals and $50,000 for all other taxpayers. The minimum penalty is $5,000 for individuals and $10,000 for all other taxpayers.

The section 6707A penalty applies even if there is no tax due with respect to the reportable transaction that has not been disclosed. There is no reasonable cause exception to the penalty. The Commissioner may, however, rescind all or a portion of a penalty, but only in the case of transactions other than listed transactions, where rescinding the penalty would promote efficient tax administration and only after the taxpayer submits a lengthy and burdensome application. In the case of listed transactions, the IRS has no discretion to rescind the penalty. The statute precludes judicial review where the Commission decides not to rescind the penalty.

The AICPA proposes for an amendment of section 6707A to allow an exception to the penalty if there was reasonable cause for the failure and the taxpayer acted in good faith for all types of reportable transactions, and to allow for judicial review in cases where reasonable cause was denied. Moreover, we propose an amendment of section 6664 to provide a general reasonable cause exception for all types of reportable transactions, irrespective of whether the transaction was adequately disclosed or the level of assurance.

9100 Relief

Section 9100 relief, which is currently available with regard to some elections, is extremely valuable for taxpayers who miss the opportunity to make certain tax elections. Congress should make section 9100 relief available for all tax elections, whether prescribed by regulation or statute. The AICPA has compiled a list[13] of elections (not all-inclusive) for which section 9100 relief currently is not granted by the IRS as the deadline for claiming such elections is set by statute. Examples of these provisions include section 174(b)(2), the election to amortize certain research and experimental expenditures, and section 280C(c), the election to claim a reduced credit for research activities. We do not believe small businesses are likely to abuse or exploit hindsight, as the IRS would continue to have discretion as to whether to grant relief for each specific request.

Form 5471 Penalty Relief

On January 1, 2009, the IRS began imposing an automatic penalty of $10,000 for each Form 5471, *Information Return of U.S. Persons with Respect to Certain Foreign Corporations*, filed with a delinquent Form 1120 series return. When imposing the penalty on corporations in particular, the IRS does not distinguish between: a) large public multinational companies, b) small companies, and c) companies that may only have insignificant overseas operations, or loss companies. This one-size-fits-all approach inadvertently places undue hardship on smaller corporations that do not have the same financial resources as larger corporations. The AICPA has submitted recommendations[14] regarding the IRS administration of the penalty provision applicable to Form 5471. Our recommendations focus on the need for relief from automatic penalties assessed upon the late filing of Form 5471 in order to promote the fair and efficient administration of the international penalty provisions of the Code.

Mobile Workforce

Another burden on small businesses that Congress should address involves the tremendous burden of tracking and complying with the many different state non-resident employee tax withholding and reporting rules for just a few days of work by an employee in a non-resident state. The state personal income tax treatment of nonresidents is inconsistent and often bewildering to multistate employers and employees.

H.R. 2315, the Mobile Workforce State Income Tax Simplification Act of 2015, introduced by Representative Bishop on May 14, 2015, addresses this issue. We are pleased that members of this Committee cosponsor this bill, and hope many others of you will also consider cosponsoring it. The AICPA strongly supports H.R. 2315 and urges Congress[15] to enact this legislation to help small businesses in this country ease their nonresident state income tax withholding and compliance burdens.

Small businesses must understand each of the states' treatment of non-resident employee withholding and assessment of taxes and the unique de *minimis* rules and definitions. Currently, 43[16] states plus the District of Columbia impose a personal income tax on wages, and there are many different requirements for withholding income tax for nonresidents among those states. There are seven states that currently do not assess a personal income tax.[17] Employees traveling into all the other states are subject to the confusing myriad of withholding and tax rules for non-resident taxpayers.

A number of states have a de *minimis* threshold, or exemption for non-residents working in the state before taxes must be withheld and paid. Others have a de *minimis* exemption based on the amount of the wages earned, either in dollars or as a percent of total income, while in the state. Further complicating the issue is that a number of these states have reciprocity agreements with other, usually adjoining, states regarding the withholding of non-resident state income taxes.

Where many businesses once tended to be local, they now have a national reach. This change has caused the operations of even small businesses to move to an interstate basis. Because of the interstate operations of these companies, many providers of services to these companies, such as certified public accountants (CPAs), find that they are also operating on an interstate basis. What once were local taxation issues have now become national in scope, and burdens must be eased in order to promote interstate commerce and ensure businesses run efficiently. These burdens take significant resources away from operating their business.

The complex filing rules impact everyone who travels for work. The recordkeeping and the requirement of having to withhold and file many state non-resident tax returns for just a few days of work in various states is overly burdensome and too complicated for both employers and employees. Additionally, the amount of research that goes into determining what each state law requires is expensive and time-consuming. A small firm or business will often be required to engage outside counsel to research the laws of the other states on an ongoing annual basis.

This issue affects all industries – retail, manufacturing, real estate, technology, food, services, etc. The current system as a whole unnecessarily creates complexity and costs for both employers and employees, without yielding a substantive benefit to most states. H.R. 2315 is needed to solve this problem and burden for small businesses.

Having a uniform national standard for non-resident income taxation, withholding, and filing requirements, as H.R. 2315 provides, will enhance compliance and significantly relieve these unnecessary administrative burdens on businesses and their employees. Additionally, H.R. 2315 provides a needed 30-day de *minimis* exemption before an employee is obligated to pay taxes to a state in which they do not reside. Many small businesses need Congress to enact this legislation.

TAX RETURN DUE DATE SIMPLIFICATION

Another challenging compliance issue for small businesses is the current illogical order of due dates for various types of tax returns. Taxpayers and preparers have long struggled with problems created by the inefficient timeline and flow of information. Federal Schedules K-1s are often delivered late, sometimes within days of the due date of taxpayers' personal returns and up to a month after the due date of their business returns. Late schedules make it difficult, if not impossible, to file a timely, accurate return. The current inefficient timeline of tax return due dates is a problem for taxpayers as well as their tax practitioners. The AICPA strongly supports this provision. It would alleviate the problems mentioned above by establishing a logical set of due dates, focused on promoting a chronologically-correct flow of information between pass-through entities and their owners. The proposal includes the changes as follows:

Current Tax Due Dates:

- March 15: S corporation and C corporation Forms 1120S and 1120; and
- April 15: Individual, Trust and Estate, and Partnership Forms 1040, 1041, and 1065

Proposed Tax Due Dates

- March 15: Partnership Form 1065;
- March 31: S corporation Form 1120S; and

- April 15: Individual, Trust and Estate, and C Corporation Forms 1040, 1041, and 1120

The provision would also revise the extended due dates to be six months after the original filing due dates for all these forms, except the trust and estate Form 1041, which would be extended five and half months.

The AICPA urges you to support this provision to change due dates for tax returns of partnerships, S corporations and C corporations because it would:

- Improve the accuracy of tax and information returns by allowing corporations and individuals to file using current data from flow-through returns that have already been filed rather than relying on estimates;
- Better facilitate the flow of information between taxpayers (i.e., corporations, partnerships, and individuals);
- Reduce the need for extended and amended tax returns; and
- Simplify tax administration for the government, taxpayers, and practitioners.

Concluding Remarks

The AICPA has consistently supported tax reform simplification efforts and permanent tax legislation because we are convinced such actions will significantly reduce taxpayers' compliance costs and encourage voluntary compliance through an understanding of the rules. The uncertainty of tax legislation creates unnecessary confusion, anxiety and administrative financial burdens. Good tax policy would promote a tax system that is balanced, economically efficient and transparent.

We encourage you to examine all aspects of the tax code to improve the current rules that have led to compliance hurdles for small businesses and administrative complexity. For example, additional relief is needed for small businesses with regards to the tangible property rules, penalty provisions need to consider their effect on voluntary compliance, and employers operating across state lines need a uniform standard on non-resident income tax withholding rules. The income tax deadlines should also promote an efficient flow of taxpayer information to provide small businesses sufficient time to file timely, accurate returns.

Finally, if small businesses are going to be allowed to grow, it is imperative that the IRS's taxpayer service issues are addressed. Small businesses and their tax preparers need to be able to contact the IRS regarding their compliance issues.

Again, Mr. Chairman, thank you for the opportunity to testify. I would be happy to answer any questions.

End Notes

[1] Small Business Administration Office of Advocacy, Frequently Asked Questions, September 2012.

[2] Commissioner Koskinen, Prepared Remarks of John A. Koskinen Commissioner, Internal Revenue Service, Before the National Press Club, dated March 31, 2015.

[3] National Taxpayer Advocate Report, Volume I: FY 2016 Objectives Report to Congress; Part II: Review of the 2015 Filing Season, dated July 14, 2015.

[4] Joint Operations Center, Customer Account Services, Account Management Paper Inventory Reports, Inventory Age Report, (Jan 1 – Apr 6 statistics).

[5] Id.

[6] National Taxpayer Advocate Report, Volume I: FY 2016 Objectives Report to Congress; Part II: Review of the 2015 Filing Season, dated July 14, 2015.

[7] Joint Operations Center, Customer Account Services, Account Management Paper Inventory Reports, Inventory Age Report, (Jan 1 – Apr 6 statistics).

[8] AICPA's Tax Policy Concept Statement No. 1: Guiding Principles for Good Tax Policy: Framework for Evaluating Tax Proposals, issued March 2001.

[9] For a detailed explanation of the differences between a compilation, a review, and an audit, please reference the AICPA Comparative Overview document.

[10] AICPA comment letter on "AICPA Tax Penalties Legislative Proposals," dated April 11, 2013; and AICPA report on "AICPA Report on Civil Tax Penalties," submitted April 11, 2013.

[11] AICPA submitted letters and written statements on Option 1 and Option 2 of Chairman Camp's Small Business Tax Reform Draft: See Option 1 comments at "AICPA testimony on Small Business and Pass-through Entity Tax Reform," dated May 17, 2013; and Option 2 comments, "AICPA Comments on Option 2 of Chairman Camp's Small Business Tax Reform Discussion Draft" dated July 30, 2013.

[12] For example, a partnership that technically terminated on April 30 of the current year due to a transfer of 80% of the capital and profits interests in the partnership to be timely filed must file its tax return for that final tax year on or before August 15 of the current year.

13 AICPA comment letter on "Tax Reform Administrative Relief for Various Statutory Elections," submitted January 23, 2015.

[14] AICPA comment letter on "Recommendations – Automatic Penalties assessments Policy with the Late Filing of Form 5471", dated March 26, 2013.

[15] AICPA written testimony before the House Committee on the Judiciary Subcommittee, Regulatory Reform, Commercial and Antitrust Law on Nexus Issues: Legislative Hearing

on H.R. 2315, The "Mobile Workforce State Income Tax Simplification Act of 2015," H.R. 1643, the "Digital Goods and Services Tax Fairness Act of 2015," and H.R. __ the "Business Activity Tax Simplification Act of 2015", dated June 2, 2015.

[16] Note that New Hampshire and Tennessee, which are included in the 43 states, do not tax wages and only subject to tax interest and dividends earned by individuals.

[17] The seven states with no personal income tax are Alaska, Florida, Nevada, South Dakota, Texas, Washington and Wyoming.

In: Small Business Tax Compliance
Editor: Sheri Patton
ISBN: 978-1-63484-565-6

Chapter 4

Statement of Stephen F. Mankowski, Partner, EP Caine & Associates, LLC. Hearing on "How Tax Compliance Obligations Hinder Small Business Growth"*

Mr. Chairman and members of the Committee, thank you for inviting me to testify today. My name is Stephen Mankowski. I am a Certified Public Accountant, member of the American Institute of CPAs (AICPA) and the National Executive Vice President and National Tax Policy Chair of the National Conference of CPA Practitioners, (*NCCPAP – the countries' second largest CPA organization). NCCPAP* is a professional organization that advocates on issues that affect Certified Public Accountants in public practice and their small business and individual clients located throughout the United States. *NCCPAP* members serve more than one million business and individual clients and are in continual communication with regulatory bodies to keep them apprised of the needs of the local CPA practitioner and its clients. Accompanying me is Ms. Sandra Johnson, National President of *NCCPAP*.

My firm has been preparing tax returns for over 30 years. My firm annually prepares well over 2,000 small business and individual tax returns as well as sales tax, payroll tax returns, highway use tax returns and 1099

* This is an edited, reformatted and augmented version of a statement presented July 22, 2015 before the House Committee on Small Business.

informational returns. We are in the trenches with clients discussing their tax, financial and personal issues, and the impact events and proposed tax law changes may have on them. Although our clients are mostly in the Pennsylvania, New Jersey and Delaware area, we serve clients in over 30 states and also provide services to clients in Canada and Europe. In this respect our practice is the same as many members of *NCCPAP* and other smaller CPA firms throughout the United States.

Tax compliance burden has been defined in the GAO report "SMALL BUSINESSES IRS Considers Taxpayer Burden in Tax Administration, but Needs a Plan to Evaluate the Use of Payment Card Information for Compliance Efforts" as the time and money spent by the taxpayer to meet tax obligations. This includes federal, state and local obligations, but NOT liabilities. The time spent on tax compliance related activities can include working with paid professionals, tax planning, record keeping, filing and submitting tax forms, learning tax laws, and working with the IRS and other jurisdictions on tax related issues. The monetary burdens can include the expenses of accounting and tax professionals, tax and accounting software, payroll services, and legal fees. An objective of the Administration and the IRS has been to minimize these burdens and eliminate unnecessary ones. For purposes of my testimony, I will simply use the term taxpayer burden to refer to tax compliance burden.

My first exposure to taxpayer burden was in November 2012. I was invited to represent *NCCPAP* and participate in an IRS panel with other tax professionals at IRS headquarters to discussed compliance burdens for both individuals and small businesses. As a CPA, I had always viewed my role as one to reduce client burden. I had not viewed my role as a source of taxpayer burden as indicated in the GAO report, which says that CPAs and tax services are part of the monetary burden of business owners. We take many of the above tasks away from the business owner to allow him/her to focus on running their business. So it is easy to see how this term can be easily mistaken. This new appreciation of what comprises taxpayer burden has allowed me to be an even better resource for my clients.

It seems that every year business owners are more in tune with how specific tax legislations could affect their business. Clients often ask how the Tax Extender legislation will affect their operations and what the Section 179 deduction limit is for the current year. While the answers tend to be similar – if you need a piece of equipment, you should buy it – that answer is not always the right answer for a business owner. Often the tax impact of the Sec. 179 deduction can be a deal-breaker. Equipment costing $100,000 could have a net cost of $60,000 with these write-offs. The $40,000 tax savings is often the deciding factor when making the purchase. While the IRS does not have control over which of the Extenders are passed, it is still a significant factor in assessing taxpayer burden.

Over the last few years, there has been a decided change in how business is conducted. As consumers have been more reluctant to carry cash, customers have forced the hand of many businesses that have historically limited payment options to cash or checks to now accept credit cards. Initially, business owners might have added a surcharge for these transactions, but with savvy consumers, credit cards and the related fees have simply become yet another cost of doing business. And another element of taxpayer burden. These business owners quickly realized that they cannot simply apply one rate for these transactions. Even after researching the processing firms to obtain the best processing rates, they learn that MasterCard and VISA have different merchant fees when compared to American Express and Discover. If the consumer uses a credit card that includes member programs or "points", an even higher processing rate may be charged by the merchant bank. In addition, there might also be monthly and compliance fees as well as equipment rental costs. And if that's not enough, the processing companies do not always deposit funds in the same manner. Most will simply deposit the gross amount of the charge and deduct the processing fees as a separate transaction. Yet many companies will deposit the net amount after deducting the processing fees, which makes the merchant's record keeping more complicated.

Most business owners have accepted these changes in how to conduct their business and accurately report their income. The IRS questioned the voluntary compliance of reporting all revenue, especially with the surge in online sales through PayPal. Under a 2008 law, the processing companies had to begin reporting credit card receipts to the IRS and the merchant in 2011 and had to add the reporting of the number of monthly transactions for 2012. This data appears on Form 1099-K, Merchant Card and Third Party Network Payments. This form must be issued once a payment processor once a merchant annually has 200 transactions and sales of at least $20,000.

Initially, the IRS had added rows onto personal returns on Schedule C and Schedule E as well as the business returns to incorporate the revenue information from Form 1099-K. However, prior to the start of the filing season, the IRS eliminated the requirement to complete these fields because too many issues arose creating much confusion. Specifically, there was confusion on how to treat sales tax, gratuities, cash back and returns on the 1099-K. Those same concerns still exist and are just some of the reasons that the IRS hasn't taken a stronger view on the use of the information on these forms.

The Form 1099-K has been a new source of taxpayer burden for the small business owner. Business owners track revenue by specific categories (i.e., sales, repairs, consulting, rent, etc.). They have not needed to track revenue based on how they are paid. Trying to accurately track revenue in the same way as the 1099-K presents data would result in an accounting nightmare. To further complicate the record keeping, businesses receive a Form 1099-K for each specific payment processor. So, if the business accepts MasterCard/VISA and American Express they would receive a form from MasterCard/VISA and one from AMEX. If they also use PayPal, they would receive a third form. If they changed their payment processing company during the year, additional forms would be received from the new processing company. The overall burden to accurately track revenue by each credit card type can be significant and generate no results that benefit the owner.

Another issue with the Form 1099-K revolved around payments for vendors that would receive a Form 1099MISC. Any payments related to these services would not be included on the Form 1099MISC. This adds a different and unique level of taxpayer burden as this would relate to both the payer and recipient. Just as businesses are not setup to track revenue by payment source, the payer would have an additional burden to exclude credit card payments from the total payment they are required to report on Form 1099MISC to the recipient.

From the IRS viewpoint, however, this form has helped increase voluntary compliance among small businesses. Many virtual businesses that had previously flown under the radar (part of the underground economy) are now filing income tax returns and paying taxes. In addition, the Form 1099-K has allowed the IRS to establish a database whereby they can obtain a better understanding of the revenue sources of a particular industry. Even though the IRS has not been able to assess taxpayers based solely on these databases, the IRS has been sending letters to taxpayers whom they feel have significantly under reported revenue. Initially, the IRS was accepting reasonable responses to these notices, but with the additional data in their databases, the IRS has a better understanding of the egregious filers, specifically those businesses reporting that 100% of their revenue was from credit card transactions.

To assist tax professionals, the IRS instituted a pilot program for the 2015 filing season called the Payment Mix Comparison Tool (PMCT). *NCCPAP* was invited to participate in the program. This program allows our members to enter selected data from the client's Form 1099-K (Merchant Category Code

(MCC), zip code, total transactions and total revenue) along with the total business income into a tool. PMCT accesses the IRS database and compares various ratios for a business with a specific MCC code against the Form 1099-K. The result tells the CPA if the results are within specifications of the database. A common flaw with the Form 1099-K is that if the payment processor applies an incorrect MCC code for a business, the PMCT results could be beyond the standard deviation which may result in an IRS notice.

The results from the PMCT have been strictly for the benefit of the taxpayer and is for informational purposes only. Currently, the IRS is not capturing data from this tool. The database will continue to improve as the volume of historical data input into the tool increases. The PMCT, unfortunately, did not get the expected usage due to a few practitioner concerns. Specifically, the name of the tool was not the best, many practitioners did not believe that the IRS was not tracking the results and the fact that PMCT did not go live until the beginning of February 2015 after most CPAs have completed their training and had already begun preparing tax returns. In addition, many felt that there should be a better result besides "typical" or "unusual" depending on where in the range their client's data fell. Hopefully, this program will continue next year and will see more usage by tax professionals. If used properly, PMCT could actually reduce taxpayer burden by addressing issues of credit card revenue while the data is still fresh in the business owner's mind.

In conclusion, taxpayer burden exists on two primary levels – time and money – to remain in compliance with today's complicated tax codes. Often, both components are viewed as one, except when contacting the IRS. Staffing and budgetary issues have resulted in longer than expected wait times and reaching IRS employees that are not able to address the caller's issues and concerns. Compliance with tax codes and dealing with new forms adds to taxpayer burden. New forms, such as Form 1099-K, are a prime example. The results may be of use to the IRS, but does not have any practical use for the business owner. Businesses do not tracked revenue by number of transactions or type of payment. Any attempt at verifying the data on the Form 1099-K would be fruitless, especially in industries, such as restaurants where customers charges often include gratuities and sales tax, neither of which are revenue to the business.

Accepting credit cards has become the norm. Most businesses historically have included all of their sales, regardless of source. With the information on Form 1099-K, the IRS now has a means to ensure that all business, especially virtual ones, are tax compliant with regard to credit card sales. With this form comes additional burdens to the taxpayer including how to reconcile sales to the revenue reported on these forms. The question that the taxpayer needs to answer is how to best run his or her business. If the business owner has systems in place to accurately track all revenue, the burden of reconciling the Form 1099-K data should be minimal. It is extremely important that the IRS has the tools to determine tax compliance and reduce the tax gap.

As various states learned that the IRS was beginning the income matching program, many decided to use this as a tool to understand the sales mix of credit cards vs. cash and checks. Currently these states have also indicated that they have no plans to use this information for audit selection or any purpose other than the collection of information. However, neither the IRS nor the participating states have assured the tax practitioners or business communities that this information will not be used in the future as a tool for audit selection despite its flaws.

This program has the potential of a disaster. This is a repeat of warnings from *NCCPAP* and others in the tax practitioner community when the Form 1099-K matching program was first proposed. It is well understood that the IRS should use all tools possible to find tax cheats. However, as the GAO has correctly indicated, this is a flawed system with no real ability of matching gross income with Form 1099-K reports. Additionally, the ratio tools now being used are very imperfect as certain assumptions used (such as NAICS codes) will skew the information.

Thank you for the opportunity to present this testimony.

INDEX

A

abuse, 79, 81
access, 35, 40, 43, 59, 62, 68, 74
accounting, 16, 19, 73, 76, 78, 79, 88, 90
activity level, 31
adverse event, 56
Alaska, 86
anxiety, 76, 84
assessment, 32, 36, 37, 38, 39, 60, 62, 82
assets, 2, 4, 7, 17, 18, 21, 43, 49, 51, 53
atmosphere, 78
audit(s), 5, 20, 21, 28, 36, 38, 41, 57, 58, 85, 92

B

balance sheet, 44
base, 74
benchmarking, 56
benefits, 24, 41, 48, 57, 58, 59, 60, 62, 63
bias, 32, 67
breakdown, 57
business partners, 8
business processes, 22
businesses, vii, 1, 2, 3, 4, 6, 8, 9, 10, 11, 13, 14, 16, 17, 18, 19, 20, 21, 26, 28, 31, 33, 35, 42, 44, 45, 46, 51, 52, 53, 66, 67, 68, 69, 74, 77, 78, 82, 83, 84, 85, 89, 90, 91

C

capital gains, 8, 9, 10, 11, 12, 43, 45, 46
cash, 27, 28, 31, 33, 34, 35, 38, 43, 89, 92
cash flow, 43
Census, 66
Chamber of Commerce, 25
classification, 18, 59, 60, 61
clients, 26, 38, 73, 87, 88
commerce, 82
communication, 38, 87
communit(ies), 5, 25, 41, 71, 92
compensation, 15
compilation, 85
complexity, 19, 26, 49, 71, 74, 76, 77, 82, 84
compliance, vii, 1, 2, 3, 4, 5, 7, 13, 14, 15, 16, 17, 18, 19, 20, 21, 23, 24, 25, 26, 27, 28, 31, 32, 33, 36, 37, 38, 40, 41, 51, 54, 56, 57, 59, 60, 63, 64, 66, 67, 68, 72, 74, 76, 77, 78, 82, 83, 84, 85, 88, 89, 90, 91, 92
conference, 40
Congress, 56, 63, 72, 74, 80, 81, 83, 85
consensus, 6
consulting, 90
consumers, 89
coordination, 63
cost, 4, 14, 16, 17, 19, 22, 26, 54, 57, 62, 63, 64, 74, 89

costs of compliance, 5
counsel, 82
culture, 23
customer service, 26, 63
customers, 23, 89, 91

D

data collection, 3, 22
database, 90, 91
decision-making process, 25
deduction, 3, 16, 24, 88
deficit, 43
delinquency, 79
Department of the Treasury, 4, 25, 63, 66, 68
Department of Transportation, 63
deposits, 15
depreciation, 3, 24, 43, 79
depth, 24
directors, 38
disaster, 92
District of Columbia, 82
draft, 39
due process, 78

E

earnings, 20, 27
economic activity, 76
economic growth, vii, 1, 4
economic progress, 4
economies of scale, 17
election, 81
e-mail, 22
employees, vii, 1, 2, 4, 6, 7, 14, 16, 17, 19, 24, 25, 42, 44, 48, 49, 52, 67, 72, 81, 82, 83, 91
employers, 10, 11, 12, 14, 15, 16, 49, 66, 69, 81, 82, 84
employment, 2, 4, 14, 15, 17, 48, 64
enforcement, 5, 26, 27, 31, 36, 39
environment, 74
equipment, 88, 89
equity, 79
Europe, 88
evidence, 3, 5, 32, 37, 38, 39, 41, 59, 63
examinations, 59, 61, 64
exclusion, 44
expenditures, 81
exposure, 88

F

faith, 78, 80
farm land, 68
farmers, 8, 10, 11, 66, 68
federal employment, 48
financial, 19, 20, 23, 49, 76, 78, 81, 84, 88
financial resources, 81
fiscal year, 23, 56, 57, 61, 64
fisheries, 19, 54
flaws, 92
focus groups, 37
food, 82
funds, 89

G

GAO, 1, 2, 3, 8, 9, 10, 11, 12, 13, 15, 18, 21, 22, 25, 28, 29, 30, 32, 34, 35, 39, 45, 46, 49, 50, 52, 53, 54, 55, 56, 58, 59, 60, 61, 62, 63, 64, 65, 66, 67, 68, 72, 88, 92
growth, vii, 1, 4, 33, 74, 76
guidance, 2, 26, 31, 40, 41, 58, 62, 63, 67, 77
guidelines, 61
guiding principles, 23, 41
guilty, 72

H

health, 16, 26, 48, 54, 67
health care, 16, 26, 48
health insurance, 48, 67
highways, 17
hiring, 7
historical data, 91

history, 73
House, 4, 71, 73, 85, 87
House of Representatives, 4

I

identification, 31, 33, 36, 38, 57, 67
identity, 76
improvements, 19
income, 2, 3, 4, 5, 6, 7, 8, 9, 10, 11, 12, 13, 14, 15, 16, 17, 20, 21, 22, 27, 28, 31, 33, 35, 40, 42, 43, 44, 45, 46, 47, 48, 49, 66, 68, 69, 73, 76, 77, 79, 81, 82, 83, 84, 86, 89, 90, 91, 92
income tax, 2, 4, 13, 14, 15, 21, 22, 47, 48, 79, 81, 82, 83, 84, 86, 90
individual taxpayers, 2, 8, 19, 20, 42
individuals, 2, 6, 14, 16, 24, 42, 68, 74, 80, 84, 86, 88
industr(ies), 2, 13, 14, 16, 19, 82, 31, 47, 49, 51, 54, 90, 91
inflation, 19, 78
information technology, 33
integration, 31
Internal Revenue Service (IRS), vii, 1, 2, 3, 4, 5, 6, 7, 13, 15, 16, 17, 18, 19, 20, 21, 22, 23, 24, 25, 26, 27, 28, 29, 30, 31, 32, 33, 34, 35, 36, 37, 38, 39, 40, 41, 43, 47, 49, 50, 51, 52, 53, 54, 55, 56, 57, 58, 59, 60, 61, 62, 63, 64, 65, 66, 67, 68, 72, 74, 75, 76, 77, 78, 80, 81, 85, 88, 89, 90, 91, 92
investment(s), 7, 32, 38, 42, 44, 57, 58, 61
issues, 7, 21, 26, 28, 61, 74, 76, 78, 82, 85, 87, 88, 89, 91

L

laws, 7, 24, 49, 66, 74, 78, 82, 88
leadership, 32, 37, 38, 74
learning, 7, 33, 35, 36, 88
legislation, 76, 81, 83, 84, 88
litigation, 35

M

magnitude, 20
majority, 8
management, 32, 33, 56
manufacturing, 82
marginal costs, 3, 18
mass, 74
measurement(s), 18, 47
Medicare, 15
membership, 75
messages, 57
methodology, 28, 31, 32, 33, 35, 37, 38, 40, 47, 51, 58, 66
mission, 23
models, 17, 19, 24, 25, 40, 47, 51, 61, 66, 67
multinational companies, 81

O

Office of Management and Budget, 17, 25
officials, 2, 5, 24, 25, 33, 35, 36, 37, 40, 41, 56, 57, 59, 61, 62, 63
operations, 14, 26, 56, 81, 82, 88
opportunities, 22, 26
organize, 49
outreach, 23, 25, 26, 33, 38, 62, 63
ownership, 6
ownership structure, 6

P

participants, 25, 48
payroll, 7, 87, 88
penalties, 75, 78, 80, 81
pension plans, 16
per capita income, 31
permit, 78
policy, 75
population, vii, 1, 2, 5, 6, 19, 22, 24, 25, 31, 33, 40, 42, 66, 67, 68
population density, 31
portfolio, 43

president, 73, 87
prevention, 79
principles, 23, 24, 77
probability, 35
professionals, 88, 90, 91
profit, 42, 74
project, 37, 38, 60
prosperity, 74
public interest, 73

R

radar, 90
RAS, 4, 40, 41
real estate, 6, 8, 9, 10, 11, 12, 42, 45, 46, 54, 68, 82
reciprocity, 82
recommendations, 26, 39, 56, 57, 58, 59, 60, 61, 62, 63, 64, 65, 72, 81
redundancy, 59
Reform, 85
regulations, 15, 62, 63, 77, 78
regulatory bodies, 87
relevance, 32, 36
reliability, 32, 36, 39, 40, 51
relief, 22, 26, 77, 78, 80, 81, 84
rent, 16, 68, 90
repair, 78
requirement(s), 6, 14, 15, 16, 17, 22, 26, 40, 49, 51, 64, 67, 74, 77, 82, 83, 89
researchers, 2, 5, 7, 19, 40, 42, 45, 46, 64, 66, 68
resources, vii, 1, 4, 23, 24, 26, 32, 33, 37, 38, 56, 57, 58, 60, 61, 63, 77, 82
response, 21, 25, 39, 56, 57, 67, 75
response time, 57, 75
restaurants, 33, 91
retail, 17, 19, 49, 82
retirement, 16, 48
revenue, 7, 28, 31, 33, 42, 89, 90, 91, 92
risk(s), 24, 25, 32, 38, 56, 60, 68, 73
risk management, 56, 73
royalty, 43
rules, 19, 37, 76, 77, 78, 81, 82, 84

S

sampling error, 42, 43, 47
savings, 24, 89
scarce resources, 57
scope, 32, 37, 56, 66, 82
Secretary of the Treasury, 39
self employment, 48
self-employed, 4, 6, 16
self-employment, 48
sensitivity, 68
services, 7, 16, 17, 56, 60, 62, 63, 73, 75, 82, 88, 90
shareholders, 6, 21, 48, 79
simulation, 51
small business(s), vii, 1, 2, 3, 4, 5, 6, 7, 8, 9, 10, 11, 12, 14, 15, 16, 17, 18, 19, 20, 22, 23, 24, 25, 26, 27, 32, 33, 35, 36, 38, 40, 41, 42, 45, 46, 47, 49, 51, 56, 57, 58, 59, 60, 61, 62, 63, 64, 66, 67, 68, 69, 71, 74, 75, 76, 77, 78, 81, 82, 83, 84, 85, 87, 88, 90
small firms, 72
Social Security, 15
software, 7, 19, 88
SOI, 4, 40, 43, 44, 68
sole proprietor, 2, 6, 8, 10, 11, 14, 16, 18, 43, 66, 68
solution, 24, 25
South Dakota, 86
specific tax, 6, 13, 47, 49, 88
specifications, 91
spending, 19
Spring, 8, 9, 10, 11, 12, 45, 46, 66, 68
staffing, 33
stakeholders, 3, 22, 23, 24, 25, 26, 32, 37, 38, 63
standard deviation, 67, 91
state(s), 7, 23, 73, 81, 82, 83, 84, 86, 88, 92
statistics, 25, 72, 85
storage, 63
strategic planning, 33

T

tax credits, 26
tax deduction, 24
tax policy, 41, 77, 78, 84
tax reform, 76, 84
tax return data, 68
tax system, 3, 76, 77, 84
taxation, 82
taxes, 4, 7, 14, 15, 16, 17, 20, 27, 47, 48, 49, 64, 71, 74, 82, 83, 90
taxpayers, 4, 5, 6, 7, 8, 9, 11, 12, 17, 20, 21, 22, 24, 27, 28, 31, 32, 33, 35, 36, 37, 38, 42, 44, 45, 46, 56, 57, 58, 59, 60, 62, 63, 64, 66, 68, 74, 75, 76, 77, 78, 80, 82, 83, 84, 90
technical comments, 39
technology, 22, 35, 82
telephone, 23, 56, 57, 58, 60, 63, 75
testing, 3, 60
theft, 76
time framc, 21, 33, 57, 60, 62, 79
total revenue, 91
trade, 19, 54
training, 33, 37, 91
transactions, 16, 27, 28, 33, 34, 35, 38, 66, 67, 80, 89, 90, 91
transcription, 59
transparency, 76, 77
Treasury, 2, 3, 4, 5, 7, 19, 25, 39, 40, 62
treatment, 8, 9, 10, 11, 12, 28, 81, 82

U

U.S. Department of the Treasury, 5, 42
U.S. economy, vii, 1, 4, 74
uniform, 83, 84
United States, vii, 1, 4, 87, 88
unstructured interviews, 41

V

variables, 31
VAT, 68
vehicles, 7, 42, 49
Vice President, 73, 87

W

wages, 15, 48, 82, 86
Washington, 56, 58, 59, 60, 61, 62, 63, 64, 65, 66, 67, 68, 72, 86
web, 22, 62
witnesses, 71, 72
workers, 15
workforce, 74
workload, 58, 59